In the Event of Laughter

Psychoanalytic Horizons

Psychoanalysis is unique in being at once a theory and a therapy, a method of critical thinking and a form of clinical practice. Now in its second century, this fusion of science and humanism derived from Freud has outlived all predictions of its demise. **Psychoanalytic Horizons** evokes the idea of a convergence between realms as well as the outer limits of a vision. Books in the series test disciplinary boundaries and will appeal to scholars and therapists who are passionate not only about the theory of literature, culture, media and philosophy but also, above all, about the real life of ideas in the world.

Volumes in the Series

Mourning Freud
Madelon Sprengnether

Does the Internet Have an Unconscious? Slavoj Žižek and Digital Culture
Clint Burnham

In the Event of Laughter: Psychoanalysis, Literature and Comedy
Alfie Bown

On Dangerous Ground: Freud's Visual Cultures of the Unconscious
Diane O'Donoghue

Born After: Reckoning with the German Past (forthcoming)
Angelika Bammer

The Analyst's Desire: Ethics in Theory and Clinical Practice (forthcoming)
Mitchell Wilson

At the Risk of Thinking: An Intellectual Biography of Julia Kristeva (forthcoming)
Alice Jardine

In the Event of Laughter

Psychoanalysis, Literature and Comedy

Alfie Bown

BLOOMSBURY ACADEMIC
NEW YORK • LONDON • OXFORD • NEW DELHI • SYDNEY

BLOOMSBURY ACADEMIC
Bloomsbury Publishing Inc
1385 Broadway, New York, NY 10018, USA
50 Bedford Square, London, WC1B 3DP, UK

BLOOMSBURY, BLOOMSBURY ACADEMIC and the Diana logo are trademarks of Bloomsbury Publishing Plc

First published in the United States of America 2019

Cover design: Daniel Benneworth-Gray
Cover image © Krzysztof Wilczynski/National Museum in Warsaw

Library of Congress Cataloging-in-Publication Data
Names: Bown, Alfie, author.
Title: In the event of laughter : psychoanalysis, literature and comedy / Alfie Bown.
Description: New York, NY : Bloomsbury Academic, 2018. |
Series: Psychoanalytic horizons | Includes bibliographical references and index.
Identifiers: LCCN 2018018976 (print) | LCCN 2018022180 (ebook) |
ISBN 9781501342646 (ePDF) | ISBN 9781501342639 (ePUB) |
ISBN 9781501342622 | ISBN 9781501342622 (hardback) |
ISBN 9781501342646 (ePDF) | ISBN 9781501342639 (eBook)
Subjects: LCSH: Laughter–Psychological aspects. | Laughter in literature. |
Comic, The, in literature. Classification: LCC BF575.L3 (ebook) |
LCC BF575.L3 B69 2018 (print) | DDC 152.4/3–dc23
LC record available at https://lccn.loc.gov/2018018976

ISBN: HB: 978-1-5013-4262-2
ePDF: 978-1-5013-4264-6
eBook: 978-1-5013-4263-9

Series: Psychoanalytic Horizons

Typeset by Newgen KnowledgeWorks Pvt. Ltd., Chennai, India
Printed and bound in the United States of America

To find out more about our authors and books visit www.bloomsbury.com and sign up for our newsletters.

Contents

Figures

Preface and Acknowledgements

Many books on comedy begin with a little anecdote about how the author had a good laugh writing the book, perhaps even starting off the discussion with a joke or two, or at least with a humorous opening gambit of some kind. Sometimes the temptation to have a laugh creeps onto the front cover of the book, making its presence felt in the illustration or in the book's subtitle, suggesting that within the book we might find a lighthearted academia that affords a much-needed relief from the all-too-serious attitudes that so often characterize the university. This is not a book which arises from this kind of atmosphere at all.

Instead, the book has come out of many years of study and academic discussion, very little of which has had the 'lightness' that we often associate with comedy, even less of which has been fun or funny, and absolutely none of which could even be said to have been a relief. If there has been a laughter ghosting the decade of reading philosophy and literature that has finally resulted in this book, it has been a threatening and unsettling laughter that has pointed to the weakness of the academy, to the fragility of philosophy and to the anxiety of my own contribution. It was the power that laughter has to be something completely opposed to a light relief, something powerfully unsettling which leaves us feeling highly anxious, which caused me to undertake this project.

A number of people deserve a special thank you for their role in these discussions and, therefore, in making this book possible. These people are, in some kind of order, Mladen Dolar, Jeremy Tambling, James Smith, David Matthews, Anca Parvulescu, Gregor Moder, Alenka Zupančič, David Alderson, Jonathan Hall, Jack Sullivan, Daniel Bristow, Ian Parker, Lucas Ballestin, Andreja Zevnik, Tony Brown and Alexandre Pais. I wish to make a special thank you to my wife Kim, without whom I would not have been able to finish this project; to my mother Tracy, without whom it would never have begun; and to my daughter Lyra, who is just beginning to laugh.

A version of Chapter 4 has appeared in *American Journal of Psychoanalysis* (July, 2017) and is included here with permission.

Note on the Text

References to Shakespeare are from *The Norton Critical Edition*, ed. Stephen Greenblatt (London: Norton, 1997).

References to Freud are from Sigmund Freud, *The Standard Edition of the Complete Psychological Works of Sigmund Freud*, ed. and trans. James Strachey et al., 24 vols (London: Vintage, 2001).

References to regularly quoted Jacques Lacan texts are as follows:

S7	*The Ethics of Psychoanalysis*, ed. Jacques Alain-Miller, trans. Dennis Porter (London: Norton, 1992).
S10	*Anxiety*, ed. Jacques Alain-Miller (Cambridge: Polity Press, 2014).
S11	*The Four Fundamental Concepts of Psychoanalysis*, ed. Jacques Alain-Miller, trans. Alan Sheridan (London: Norton, 1998).
S17	*The Other Side of Psychoanalysis*, ed. Jacques Alain-Miller, trans. Russel Grigg (London: Norton, 2007).

Introduction: Laughter's Doubleness

Imitation of laughter and (the devil's) original laughter are both called by the same name.

Milan Kundera[1]

We all enjoy a good laugh. But is laughter purely and completely enjoyable? Whether we see laughter as a liberating release or as a tool for social control, we rarely question the fact that laughing feels good. The 'positive' feeling we often get from laughter may have its roots in social, biological or psychological conditions, or in a combination of all three. What is sometimes called 'nervous laughter' is perhaps the exception, a laughter that is not seen as inherently or at least entirely enjoyable. Yet, it is not difficult to suggest that there is anxiety within every laugh, or that when we laugh, anxiety is never far away. Laughter is joyful and expressive, even celebratory, but it is also unsettling and disconcerting, and it often leaves us feeling unsure of ourselves. When we are in the midst of throes of laughter we can feel confident, free and assured, but a deep anxiety often follows closely on the tail of these affects. A whole history of art and literature, in its multiple depictions of laughter and laughing subjects, has picked up on this uneasy doubleness, showing laughter as simultaneously horrifying and full of delight. It is this doubleness that makes laughter so difficult to study and so elusive and hard to pin down. In short, this book is an attempt to explore why and how laughter is so paradoxically worrying and pleasurable.

Several centuries of philosophical study and infinitely more hours of general discussion, not to mention scientific and psychological investigations, have asked the question of *why* we laugh and of what *causes* laughter. Every discussion of why a particular joke is funny is a different attempt to answer this question. By contrast, very little attention has ever been dedicated to thinking about laughter's *effects*, to what is happening to us when we laugh and to how

[1] Milan Kundera, *The Book of Laughter and Forgetting*, trans. Alan Asher (London: Faber and Faber, 1996), p. 87.

experiencing laughter might affect or change us. Some recent work, most notably Anca Parvulescu's *Laughter*, has broken from this mould and focussed on what the experience of laughter does to us as subjects. This work shows how laughter can have social and historical effects which may sometimes be more important than asking what caused it. But, my concern here is not so much to work out specific causes *or* effects of laughter. Rather, I argue in this book that laughter can call into question the relationship between *cause* and *effect* and that this is what lies behind how troubling and unsettling it can be to laugh. Laughter can sometimes seem to be the act of a most secure individual, a Hobbesian 'glory' of self-celebration. It can also, since it is a group activity, be what Jonathan Hall calls a 'fascist joy' involving 'collaboration with the powerholders'.[2] Yet there is, at least most often and perhaps ultimately always, a remainder or leftover in laughter that leaves us feeling troubled. This book is about this elusive and sometimes almost imperceptible and indefinable residue found in laughter that leaves us ruffled.[3]

To be more specific, at the heart of this book I explore the relationship between laughter and anxiety by arguing that laughter should be thought of in terms of what the French philosopher and psychoanalyst Alain Badiou calls the 'event'. This puts laughter in a radical position from which it can unseat and threaten many of the foundations of our ideology. 'Ideology' is used in something like the Althusserian sense here, as that which turns 'concrete individuals' into 'concrete subjects'.[4] Loosely, we can say that ideology is something like the 'official' way in which we are encouraged to see ourselves as subjects and the ways in which we are encouraged to relate to other people and things. This official world, I argue, is often erected and supported by laughter, but it can also be threatened and challenged by the process of laughing. However, this 'radical' capacity of laughter, if it can be called that, is very different to any existing investments in the radical potential of laughter and comedy, of which there are a great many. Existing discussions of laughter are politically dangerous, and this book offers an analysis of these dangers and suggests an alternative framework for discussing the role of laughter in our social structure. It argues that the role laughter plays in a unique space between politics and entertainment is in need of a new kind of attention. Seeing laughter in terms of the Badiouian 'event' means seeing it as a force that

2 Jonathan Hall, *Anxious Pleasures* (London: Associated University Press, 1995), p. 17.

3 By contrast the most famous theorist of laughter Henri Bergson claims that laughter only 'falls on the surface of a soul that is thoroughly calm and unruffled'. See Henri Bergson, *Laughter: An Essay on the Meaning of the Comic*, trans. Cloudesely Brereton and Fred Rothwell (Rockville: Arc Manor, 2008), p. 10.

4 Louis Althusser, *Lenin and Philosophy and Other Essays*, trans. Ben Brewster. (New York: Monthly Review Press, 2001), p. 116.

erects and constructs ideologies and subjectivities, but simultaneously calls these very things into question. This book therefore offers not an alternative interpretation of what laughter is, nor another answer to the question of why we laugh, but an alternative framework for discussing laughter that escapes, I hope, some of the problems that characterize existing discussions.

The idea of reading laughter as 'the event' is not something that Alain Badiou himself would be likely to agree with, and so this book should not be thought of as an application of Badiou's theory in a new context – the context of laughter. For Badiou, there are four kinds of 'event', and laughter is far from being one of them. A Badiouian event is a rare and unusual occurrence, something that occasionally interrupts the trajectory of things and reorders the world around it. Arguing that laughter is an 'event' means seeing this process very differently – as something that occurs a great many times each day to a great many people and in a great many different ways. The book therefore involves rethinking the 'event' itself.

In short, seeing laughter as 'event' means recognizing that part of laughter's *effect* is the power to retroactively change its *causes*. The effect of laughter modifies the thing laughed at (the object of laughter) and it modifies the person laughing (the subject of laughter). An example would be to show the role of jokes in constructing national identities, rather than seeing a joke as something that merely reinforces or reflects existing nationalisms. These jokes, while routed in existing nationalist ideologies, also exceed and change the discourse, creating new nationalisms. In his book *Event*, Slavoj Žižek defines the event as '*the effect that seems to exceed its causes*'.[5] An 'event' is a moment of excess, so that while it has political stimuli, it also establishes new causes for itself, its effects retroactively restructuring the past into a new structure and bringing us within this reordered world, whether we like it or not.[6] In other words, laughter brings the subjects involved (those telling the jokes, those laughing and those targeted) into new ideological structures which are produced, entrenched, naturalized and enforced by the process of laughter. This means that laughter can be radical or conservative, ideological or liberating, leftwing or rightwing, depending on the structures it responds to and reconstructs. It also means that laughter always contains the possibility to unsecure, showing how precarious subjectivity is. Laughter, I argue throughout this book, is an event that constructs and controls us, but it is

5 Slavoj Žižek, *Event: Philosophy in Transit* (London: Penguin Books, 2014), p. 3.

6 From this point on, I have dropped the quotation marks from the word event, which is used only in this Badiouian sense in what follows. Broadly speaking, the term event designates an occurrence which changes not only the present and the future but the past as well.

also an event which undermines and makes visible these very constructions and controls.

The origins of this particular concept of the event (distinct from other philosophical treatments of it) are found in the psychoanalytic concept of *nachträglichkeit*, sometimes translated as 'afterwardsness'. Nachträglichkeit is deferred action, or retroactive action. Rather than a later reaction to an earlier event, nachträglichkeit is a recognition that when an event occurs, earlier events are invested with new significances so that the past is transformed into that which it will then always already have been. Ian Parker puts it clearly:

> This is a peculiarly psychoanalytic conception of time, a looping back and activation of what has already occurred, and the investment of that first event with a significance that turns it into what it will later always already be.[7]

Laughter ought to be read in light of this, in order to explore how it changes the place into which it erupts, reorganizing the world but making it appear as though things have always been that way, as if laughter was merely a response to what was already there. Yet, in threatening to reveal this to us, laughter retains an anxious signal that our reality is so easily reordered and reconstructed. What we might call laughter's 'evental' capacity is usually ignored: we see laughter only as a response or symptom, an effect of something 'funny'. A two-page article in a special humour edition of *Philosophy Now* in 2016 made the unsettling point that nothing is funny until it is qualified as such when we laugh at it.[8] There is something like a paradox here, since something must be funny in order to stimulate the laughter that qualifies the joke or object as funny. This point raises a problem in conceptualization of laughter, and a full theory of laughter as event is needed to negotiate it.

Alongside this, the other main project of the book is to trace the conceptualization of the event through its history in psychoanalysis and Hegelianism, showing that while the philosophical concept of the event has not been directly connected to comedy by any of the most important philosophers to develop the idea, laughter has never been far away from the theory of the event. Many philosophers have conceptualized the event, including Heidegger, Foucault, and Deleuze, as well as the theorists on whom this book focusses. While many of these philosophers are discussed in this

[7] Ian Parker and David Pavon-Cuellar, 'Lacanian Domains of Practice and Forms of Event in Analysis', in *Lacan, Discourse, Event* (London: Routledge, 2013), pp. 338–46 (p. 338).

[8] Alan Soble, 'Nothing Is Funny but Laughing Makes It So', *Philosophy Now*, no. 111 (December 2015/January 2016), pp. 8–10.

book, it is the particular Badiouian idea of the event that is central to the theorization of laughter presented here. This idea has its roots in Badiou's synthesis of Hegelianism and Lacanian psychoanalysis. While it might be said that Badiou's idea of retroactivity, developing from psychoanalysis, is an interruption to Hegelian dialectical time or time as forward-moving and progressive, the germs of this interruption can also be found in Hegel's work itself. The argument here traces this unique conceptualization of the event from its origins in Hegel to its culmination in the work of Badiou.

Laughter ghosts the work of Hegel, Freud, Lacan and Badiou as this concept of the event develops, and the book picks up on this key link between laughter and the event and then reads laughter back in light of the connection. This shows the political significance of these discussions and of laughter. We live in a society characterized by what Mark Fisher, borrowing from Frederic Jameson and Žižek, calls 'capitalist realism', meaning that contemporary ideology makes it appear that capitalism is completely inevitable. By showing laughter's 'evental capacity' to make the realities it establishes seem inevitable, we unsecure this apparent inevitability of things. Ultimately we get a glimpse into how dominant thought is able to construct itself as unavoidable, and we see that it often does so through laughter. In this reading, laughter is shown to be perhaps the single most powerful ideological tool, a force that constructs the relations between people and things and makes those relations seem natural. Yet, because of this, it is also a site at which we can see this process happening, unsecuring the very ideologies brought into being.

There are four chapters in the main body of the book, each of which is divided into two parts. The first part of each chapter is dedicated to the theorization of laughter as well as to the analysis of how and why laughter has been theorized in the way it is. The second part of each chapter is dedicated to a literary example, which is not used to so much bear out the theory (though at times it does) but to problematize existing ideas in comic theory and to suggest other dimensions to laughter that have been hitherto ignored by studies of comedy. Rather than jokes, the examples used are all what could be called 'literary' examples of comedy. There are various reasons for this. Each example is a case of sustained narrative in which not only the reader but the characters are stimulated into laughter. This allows for an assessment of the various subject-positions involved when laughter arises, from the targets and objects of laughter to the subjects causing laughter, to those more imaginary audiences to the scenes of comedy, such as the reader or viewer both at the time of writing and in the present. While one could object that literary laughter is fictional, it nevertheless provides a site at which the various effects of laughter on subjectivity can be explored. Furthermore, since authors always impose their own (conscious and/or unconscious) interpretations on the laughter they describe, the important connections between what laughter *actually* does and those who use laughter *think* it does can be made visible by exploring possible gaps between the intended and actual effects of laughter. In his 1927 essay 'Humour', Freud notes the importance of literature in conceptualizing humour in general:

> Humour arises when a writer or a narrator describes the behaviour of real or imaginary people in a humorous manner. There is no need for those people to display any humour themselves; the humorous attitude is solely the business of the person who is taking them as his object. (*SE 21*: 161)

Freud continues to explore how humour 'can be directed either towards the subject's own self or towards other people' and also how the 'non-participating onlooker' derives a different but comparable yield of pleasure to the humourist themselves (*SE 21*: 163). Literature, with its various subject-positions of humourists, onlookers and targets, is the space through which the structures of laughter can be most effectively assessed. Mikhail Bakhtin felt that literature had inherited the carnival's role in modern times, and if this is so then its carnivalesque or 'overturning' capacity can be found not in its ability to 'free' us from political structures but in its ability to make those structures visible to us. Literature can reveal to us laughter's hidden effects on all the subjects involved, from reader to writer to character.

The first two chapters discuss trends in what has been variously called comic theory, laughter studies and humour studies, as well as trends in general discussions of laughter and the language used to discuss and conceptualize laughter. The third chapter is the largest and most central one, which discusses the idea of laughter as an event in full and traces the relationship between the event and laughter. The fourth chapter returns to the subject with which the book opened – the relationship between laughter and anxiety. It argues that the theory of laughter as event ultimately explains the anxiety present (whether visible or hidden) within all laughter. Finally, the conclusion discusses the idea of a 'history of laughter' in light of these discussions.

Laughter studies

Although there is a vast amount of work on various forms of comedy, there is no direct or clear community of 'laughter studies' or even 'comedy studies'.

The relatively new journal *Comedy Studies* brings together material on comedy in a largely UK context, while the reputable German journal *Humor* is the biggest regular publication in what it calls the 'field of humor studies'. Quite separate to this is the groundbreaking body of work put out on comedy in recent years by the Slovenian Lacanian school of philosophy, which is discussed in detail in Chapter 2. Books and articles on comedy are most often absent from each other's bibliographies, and the relatively scattered academic conferences on comedy tend to feature different speakers each time. If we can speak of an academic body of work on laughter then this is a newly emerging body which this book aims to help bring together in the hope that further studies of comedy and laughter can develop. In my further discussions and in the bibliography to this book I have tried to bring together a variety of work on comedy and laughter that has not been in conversation before.

In some ways, with laughter we are treating one of the most general subjects of all, since laughter is something almost everyone experiences (though not perhaps *absolutely* everyone, as I discuss later). At least since Aristotle argued that it marks the difference between man and animal (an early version of 'we all enjoy a good laugh'), laughter has been seen as a universal human trait, something that we all share in.[9] This idea has continued throughout history, and the idea that man is the only animal who laughs has resurfaced in almost every century since Aristotle's famous claim.[10] Yet, just because all (or most) humans experience laughter, there is no reason to assume that all humans experience it in the same way, or even that any two humans experience it in the same way, or even that any two laughs by a single human are the same experience. Laughter is particularly troubling to human identity because it seems so different in each case, and because it often seems to powerfully divide people. While we have an impulse to celebrate laughter for bringing people together, we also know that it can be cruel, divisive and alienating. It may even be that we have often dealt with this anxiety about laughter's divisive and alienating functions by proclaiming that laughter is a particularly human thing in order to sustain the illusion that it unifies rather than divides the human experience. Laughter may be Anti-Humanist.

9 Aristotle, *On the Parts of Animals I–IV*, trans. James G. Lennox (Oxford: Oxford University Press, 2001), p. 69. On this theory of laughter in Greek culture, see Stephen Halliwell, 'The Uses of Laughter in Greek Culture', *Classical Quarterly*, vol. 41, no. 2 (1991), pp. 279–96.

10 William Hazlitt remarks in 1819, for example, that 'man is the only animal that laughs'. See his *Lectures on the English Comic Writers* (London: Taylor and Hessey, 1819), p. 1. Henri Bergson gives the modern version of this idea in his essay *Laughter*, discussed further later, where he claims that man is the only laughable animal, in the sense that man is the true 'object' of laughter. On this, see Anca Parvulescu, *Laughter: Notes on a Passion* (Cambridge, MA: MIT Press, 2010), p. 4.

Despite the fact that every laugh may be different, the idea of laughter as universal has affected the way it has been discussed and theorized, and many contributors to the discussion have written as if to speak universally for every laugh and every 'laugher'. I use the term 'laugher' in this book, a term that Kafka used, to refer to the subject found laughing in any given instance. For the sake of clarity I have retained the punctuation marks for each use of the word to prevent the easy confusion with laughter, which refers to the more abstract idea of laughter not necessarily connected with a subject. In much criticism, laughter has been treated broadly and generally, with a focus on how all laughter can be explained in one or a few swoops. This obviously assumptive trend is embodied by Murray Davis's position, though there are countless examples that could have been quoted in its place:

> I will study instances of humour less to discover the features of our specific society that led to their special creation than to discover the abstract universal properties of society that allow the creation of humour in general.[11]

Such a view risks generalizing and subsuming a great variety of laughters under one heading (in this case that of 'humour') and implies that we might be able to explain the function or cause of laughter across the board and 'in general'. To some extent working against this idea that laughter can be treated 'in general' is an existing body of work on the comedy of individual writers and artists, from Shakespeare and Jonson through Fielding and Swift, to Beckett, Chaplin, The Marx Brothers, Woody Allen, etc. These projects have usually insisted, not wrongly, that the subject of the study in question is unique and individual, personally, historically or both.[12] They have therefore resisted the idea that laughter can be treated broadly or in general terms, often arguing for the specifically radical or interesting laughter of their chosen comedian. Such texts make laughter the opposite of universal. Indeed, in a room full of people laughing, each may be laughing differently, laughing at different moments, at different things and

[11] Murray S. Davis, *What's So Funny? The Comic Conception of Culture and Society* (Chicago: Chicago University Press, 1993), p. 31.

[12] An exhaustive list would be impractical, but some individual studies of comic figures that I would like to give reference to are Laura Salisbury, '"SO THE UNREASONING GOES": The Comic Timing of Trembling', *Ill Seen Ill Said, Samuel Beckett Today*, vol. 11 (2001), pp. 373–81; Mladen Dolar, 'Comedy and Its Double', in *Schluss mit der Komodie! Zue sch,leichenden Vorherrschaft des Tragischen in unserer Kultur (Stop That Comedy! On the Subtle Hegemony of the Tragic in Our Culture)*, ed. Robert Pfaller (Wien: Slonderzahl, 2005), pp. 181–210; Malcolm Andrews, *Dickensian Laughter: Essays on Dickens and Humour* (Oxford: Oxford University Press, 2013).

even in different ways even while their laughs may appear to be directed at the same things at the same moment. Some examples are obvious cases of this, as when children's comedies have a double meaning hidden from young viewers so that adults laugh at the jokes differently. It is not uncommon to discuss comedy and find that the people in the discussion were stimulated to laughter for quite different reasons. It may even be that when a large group of people respond collectively to a single joke, no two people are laughing in precisely the same way.

Yet, this is not a particularly important or politically useful thing to say, and there are limitations of this insistence on the uniqueness of each laugh. One of the most powerful things about laughter is that it *can* be broad and affect a great many people ideologically. In fact, in thinking about laughter's social and political effects it is clear that the differences between people's laughter are less important than the similarities. The ideological effects of laughter are, of course, various. Among other things, laughter can create and reinforce prejudice, it can produce the appearance of freedom or spontaneity and it can group people together or alienate people from each other. If laughter reinforces prejudice, for example, it is important when this laughter is experienced by large groups, even if there may be small differences between the reactions of each individual. In cases such as this, the connections between our laughs are more important than the differences between them or the unique qualities of each laugh or type of laughter. While each laugh might indeed be different, it is laughter's role as a group activity that is most in need of study and which can reveal the most powerful politics of laughter's effects. Noting that every laugh is different may not be wrong, but it neglects the ways in which laughter's power over us is usually a collective one. Likewise, claiming to speak about all laughter clearly neglects its various and diverse effects. In short, it is insufficient to speak of either all laughter or of just one unique instance of laughter, and we need another way of discussing the matter.

Laughter or comedy, heaviness and light

A decision has already been made with the choice of 'laughter' over 'comedy' as the central subject of discussion. There are two main reasons for this, the first of which is relatively straightforward. My interest is in the laugh itself and in moments of laughter, rather than in the tradition of Comedy as a genre that is usually opposed to Tragedy.[13] The book discusses comedy, jokes

[13] See the discussions of comedy in Leo Salingar, *Shakespeare and the Tradition of Comedy* (Cambridge: Cambridge University Press, 1974); for an approach to Comedy as genre

and comic writing as moments which are related to laughter, which can cause laughter and which are defined by the laughter they cause. This is an important difference of emphasis: it is often the strange or anachronistic effect of laughter which is not in line with the conventions and traditions surrounding it that is most interesting and important. While laughter refers to various incidences, comedy and humour refer to sets of conventions and ideas. In his interesting and neglected book *The Sense of Humour* (1954), Stephen Potter writes that while 'humour' is a specific thing referring to what we call 'comedy', laughter comes from everywhere: there is the laugh at something funny, but there is also 'the laugh which fills a blank in conversation … the laugh to attract attention … the laugh [of] the new arrival in the hall, the laugh of the lone man at the theatre … the laugh of creative pleasure [and] the laugh of relief from physical danger'.[14] We might say that while comedy is a specific form, laughter appears to be *formless*; every laugh, it seems, is different, and it is not always easy to see any connection between one laugh and the next. As mentioned earlier, the task can be looking for the less visible of these connections, the ones not explained by conventions of comedy and humour. The second and not unrelated reason for choosing laughter over comedy as the primary subject is that, as a theory of laughter, this book attempts to move away from a number of trends in existing discussions of 'comedy'. As suggested earlier, it takes a different approach to laughter, asking not what constitutes the comic or what makes something funny, but instead how we can think in new ways about what transformations take place when we laugh. While the genre of comedy has long been taken seriously, the experience of laughter is usually neglected.

As I have intimated, although there are a number of books on comedy and a few more recent 'overview' books or introductions to the theory and/or history of comedy, there is little sense of discussion between these individuals. However, this is not to say that work on comedy has been fragmented and disconnected. On the contrary, the history of theorizing laughter has suffered from the dominance of a number of trends and assumptions that are made about laughter. Unlike comedy and laughter itself, which (we tend to believe) tend towards discontinuity and fragmentation, discussions of comedy have been organized by sets of assumptions and by dominant ideas about what laughter does. In short, the age-old question of those discussing comedy has been that of why we laugh, or of what we laugh at. As a result, discussions have focused on laughter as an 'effect' of a 'cause' which precedes the event

rather than laughter which engaged with this discussion see John Morreall, *Comedy, Tragedy and Religion* (Albany: SUNY Press, 1999), p. 13.

14 Stephen Potter, *The Sense of Humour* (London: Penguin Books, 1954), pp. 25–6.

of the laugh itself; laughter is always caused by something which 'explains' it. Usually, finding out what causes laughter is where the discussion stops. Charles Gruner's 1997 book *The Game of Humour*, for example, carries with it the subtitle 'A Comprehensive Theory of Why We Laugh'.[15] This focus on what is funny and why it is funny is almost all-pervasive in discussions of laughter, and the majority of the studies discussed in what follows are variations of this position; they have all searched for the origins or causes of laughter.

Another of these controlling assumptions is the fact that comedy ought to be treated 'lightly' or is considered something which itself involves treating things lightly (as in the phrase 'to make a joke of it'). It is hoped that if this book proves just one thing it is that there could not be a more serious matter than laughter. Mikhail Bakhtin has foregrounded the problem that it is wrong to see laughter as apolitical, and that if it is overturning, liberating or disruptive (see Chapter 1), this is only so relationally; laughter's meaning is inseparable from its political context. Far from being a departure from the political or serious, laughter is deeply bound up with ideology, something we rarely confront. Proving this point, sociologist Erving Goffman has shown that 'only joking' is one of the most common phrases in the English language. Each utterance of the phrase is an act of dismissal that frames the material involved in a particular way and controls the effect it has, suggesting that we should not attach much importance to moments of comedy.[16] This relies upon the idea that laughter is apolitical or even harmless: if we dismiss something as comic it is to be taken less seriously and seen as something that is not damaging and dangerous. This is a strange kind of Freudian 'disavowal', a term which fits into the schema 'I know very well, but all the same'. As Octave Mannoni puts it, disavowal is a coping mechanism for life; in the most general schema, it runs: 'I know very well that life is finite – not only my life, but *all* life – but all the same I carry on with things.'[17] This sort of mechanism is in play with our treatment of laughter: we know fully well that laughter is serious, dangerous, cruel and ideological, and in some conversations we openly admit this, but then we continue to treat laughter 'lightly', we make light of things using humour and we see comedy as an apolitical relief from serious things.

15 Charles Gruner, *The Game of Humour: A Comprehensive Theory of Why We Laugh* (London: Transaction, 2000).
16 See Erving Goffman, *Frame Analysis* (New York: Harper, 1974).
17 Octave Mannoni, 'I Know Well, but All the Same…', trans. G. M. Goshgarian, in *Perversion and the Social Relation*, ed. Molly Anne Rothenberg, Dennis A. Foster and Slavoj Žižek (Durham: Duke University Press, 2003), p. 70.

Discussing this point, French philosopher Gilles Lipovetsky has hypothesized that we are living in a 'humoristic society'. For Lipovetsky, the humour disseminated in contemporary society demands that we be *light* and 'easy', which can be a way to encourage consumption and consumerism.[18] Though such ideas can be useful when discussing capitalism, they rely on certain assumptions about laughter. The relationship between capitalism and laughter is an important topic, and Lipovetsky makes some important arguments here, but my position is a different one. If a 'humoristic' society is one in which we take things 'easy' and 'lightly', then a supposition has been made about the status of comedy. Later I make the case that this assumption can be a particularly important one: laughter can impose ideology in particularly powerful ways *because* it seems to be light, easy and apolitical. In other words, it is not that we ought to take social life less humoristically, but that we ought to take humour more seriously. The question of lightness is also a topic for Milan Kundera and the problem he points to in *The Unbearable Lightness of Being* – the assumption that lightness is positive, whereas heaviness, with its association with melancholia, is negative. Kundera asks, 'is heaviness truly deplorable and lightness splendid?' He interrogates, in relation to Nietzsche, the idea that lightness is so strangely invested in uncritical positivity, and we can clearly see that laughter suffers from this investment too. Laughter, we uncritically assume, is good for us, as commonplaces such as 'its good to laugh' and 'laughter is the best medicine' illustrate. Among other questions we need to ask: Is laughter truly splendid? Might not the fact that laughter is assumed to be splendid and light be a part of its powerful ability to control and organize us in particular ways?

While on the subject of laughter and medicine, I want to note that despite this being a book very much grounded in the arts and specifically in the literature and philosophy departments of the university, a body of scientific work on humour and laughter has been consulted in the course of the project.[19] Generally speaking, this research has shown at the very least that the idea of laughter as positive is another of the existing assumptions that a new discussion of comedy should leave behind. While some scientific work on laughter has maintained the line that laughter is inherently good for you, more recent work, though sometimes still within a positivist discourse, has

[18] See Gilles Lipovetsky, *The Empire of Fashion: Dressing Modern Democracy*, trans. Catherine Porter (Princeton: Princeton University Press, 1994), p. 199.

[19] For some who have argued for humour's positive effects, see G. E. Vaillant, 'Adaptive Mental Mechanisms: Their Role in a Positive Psychology', *American Psychologist*, vol. 55 (2000), pp. 89–98; H. M. Lefcourt and R. A. Martin, *Humor and Life Stress: Antidote to Adversity* (New York: Springer-Verlag, 1986); and R. A. Martin, *The Psychology of Humor: An Integrative Approach* (Burlington, MA: Elsevier Academic Press, 2007).

found clear evidence that laughter should not always be seen as positive or healthy, arguing instead for its negative effects.[20] Recent scientific studies have pointed out this problem and acknowledged that the blind cultural investment in laughter as positive is potentially dangerous.[21] Thus, while this scientific material will be left behind in what follows and is by no means my area of expertise, it is worth pointing out that what we might call the philosophical or cultural approach of this book is not in contradiction with current scientific studies of laughter. Given that comedy studies have been attentive to the dangers of laughter, at least since Thomas Hobbes and his idea of laughter as caused by a cruel assertion of superiority, it is surprising that so much discourse around laughter, particularly in cultural and literary studies, should still be unquestionably on the side of laughter as positive.[22] At the very least, laughter is just as often bad as it is good, whatever we mean by those terms.

In *The Book of Laughter and Forgetting*, quoted as an epigraph to this chapter, Kundera writes of the doubleness in laughter:

> Nowadays we don't realize that the same external display (that of laughter) serves two absolutely opposed internal attitudes. There are two laughters, and we have no word to tell one from the other.[23]

Kundera puts this doubleness in terms of angelic and demonic laughter, writing that the angel's 'imitation of laughter and (the devil's) original laughter are both called by the same name'. For Kundera, 'whereas the devil's laughter denotated the absurdity of things', the angel's laughter, on the contrary, 'meant to rejoice over how well ordered, wisely conceived, good, and meaningful everything here below was'.[24] For Kundera, angelic laughter is a light-hearted laughter that believes in beauty and fixed meaning in an ordered social world, a laughter which maintains the order of things. Yet, for Kundera, this is only half of laughter's work, only one of its faces, only one of the forces designated by the word 'laughter'. On the other side is demonic laughter, which reflects

[20] For scientific studies demonstrating the negative effects of laughter, see K. M. Lehman, K. L. Burke, R. Martin, J. Sultan and D. R. Czech, 'A Reformulation of the Moderating Effects of Productive Humor', *Humor: International Journal of Humor Research*, vol. 14 (2001), pp. 131–61.

[21] See Andrea C. Samson and James J. Gross, 'Humour as Emotion Regulation: The Differential Consequences of Negative Versus Positive Humour', *Cognition & Emotion*, vol. 26, no. 2 (2012), pp. 375–84.

[22] One area in which this has not been the case is work on laughter and disability, which consisted of only three major studies. See most recently the *Journal of Literary & Cultural Disability Studies* issue on 'Disability, Humour and Comedy', ed. Tom Coogan and Rebecca Mallett, vol. 7, no. 3 (2013) which outlines the work done in the field.

[23] Kundera, *Book of Laughter and Forgetting*, p. 87.

[24] Ibid.

the absurdity of things, perhaps overturning or overthrowing, or perhaps simply *changing* things – a laughter that, far from simply reasserting existing orders and structures, reorders and restructures the world.

For Kundera, to call this demonic laughter 'original', as compared with the angel's 'imitative' laughter, is important. Agnes Heller has suggested that 'one can even dare to say that the same joke is never told twice', on account of the differences in each telling of a joke.[25] In such a reading, every joke and every laugh is original. Opposed to this idea, Kundera wants to contrast an imitative and repetitious laughter that angelically keeps things in order with a demonic original laughter that has a more transformative power. Only demonic, 'original' laughter can change things, while angelic imitations of laughter simply repeat existing structures and reaffirm them. Canned laughter on television would be the most perfect example of angelic laughter, a laugh that is anticipated and understood a priori to its moment of apparent eruption.[26] This is a useful framework for discussions of humour, and it can be productive to discuss which of these categories any given example of laughter falls into. Somewhat anachronistically, Charles Dickens's novel *Little Dorrit* (1857) picks up on this angelic imitative laughter and its role in simply reinscribing social relations. The novel makes a point of emphasizing two characters who take the world 'lightly', indicating the angelic humour that they are likely to employ. The character Henry Gowan has a 'characteristic balancing of his which reduced everything in the wide world to the same light weight' and would fit perfectly with Lipotvesky's theory of laughter or with Kundera's angelic lightness.[27] Then there is the aristocrat Lord Decimus, a man fully on the side of stability and maintaining the existing order of things, who tells the same joke over and over again:

> Lord Decimus had a reminiscence about a pear-tree formerly growing in a garden near the back of his dame's house at Eton, upon which pear-tree the only joke of his life perennially bloomed. It was a joke of a compact and portable nature.[28]

This imitative laughter which is 'compact' and 'portable' is 'the only joke' of Lord Decimus's life, told and retold in various contexts to the same effect, embodying perfectly Kundera's angelic imitative laughter. It is hardly significant if Lord

25 Agnes Heller, *Immortal Comedy: The Comic Phenomenon in Art, Literature and Life* (Oxford: Lexington Books, 2005), p. 127.
26 For more on canned laughter, see Mladen Dolar, *The Enjoying Machine in Penumbra*, ed. Sigi Jöttkandt and Joan Copjec (Melbourne: re:press, 2013), pp. 85–105.
27 Charles Dickens, *Little Dorrit*, ed. Helen Small (London: Penguin, 2003), p. 330.
28 Ibid., p. 588.

Decimus tells the joke slightly differently each time or whether it changes depending on the context of its deployment (as Heller might emphasize). It is rather more important that this repetitious and imitative laughter reinscribes existing positions and relations. Kundera may take this argument from that of Charles Baudelaire, who, in his essay 'On the Essence of Laughter', writes that it is not difficult to 'find a certain unconscious pride at the core of the laughter's thought'.[29] Such laughter simply reaffirms the superiority of one over another. But in the category of 'the absolute comic', he sees another potential in laughter. While for Baudelaire 'the comic is an imitation', 'the absolute comic' is 'a creation'.[30] One laughter creates, while another merely imitates. Whether these two laughters are as distinct as Kundera and Baudelaire make out, or whether both elements may often be bound within the same laugh, is a major consideration of what follows. What we can take from this is the clear sense that the diabolical power of laughter is often hidden in our laughter, if not entirely lost, leaving us with jokes that work much more like Lord Decimus's does, in complete support of existing order. Anca Parvulescu has used Norbet Elias's theory of 'the civilizing of laughter' to suggest that the burst or break of laughter materially looked different in the sixteenth century when compared to the twentieth century, where even facial expressions accompanying laughter are increasingly controlled, less contorted and ultimately less demonic.[31] In a sense, this book is investigating the ideological counterpart of this suggestion: whether laughter itself has lost its demonic edge.

Kundera's work implies a religious framework, as the terms 'angelic' and 'demonic' suggest, and his writing carries the traces of the Cold War, which is a more specific context to the broader approach to laughter in this book. Here I am not interested in laughter in strictly religious terms, and my chosen examples of laughter reach far outside this historical context. However, the terms set out by Kundera, and echoed in Baudelaire, take us into the important consideration of whether these two forces of laughter are to be found in two separate instances of laughter or whether both 'angelic' and 'demonic' forces can be found dialectically within the same laugh.

Though religion is not the subject matter here, to discuss a laughter that maintains social order is to touch upon the strange connection between laughter and Christianity, as Kundera's terminology implies. In this area of philosophy, the most bizarre and strange book, which is also the authority on the topic, is *Laughter at the Foot of the Cross*, written by M. A. Screech.

[29] Charles Baudelaire, 'On the Essence of Laughter', in *The Painter of Modern Life and Other Essays* (London: Phaidon Press, 2006), pp. 147–65 (p. 152).

[30] Ibid., p. 157.

[31] Parvulescu, *Laughter*, p. 24.

The book intriguingly and unconventionally explores how 'at the foot of the Cross, as Jesus hung in agony, the crowd laughed'. For Screech, as a result of this, Christians have always been ambivalent about laughter. He writes:

> There have always been Christians who feel ill at ease with happy laughter: 'can it', they wonder, 'have any place at all in an evil, unjust, faithless, suffering world?' Yet evil, injustice, heresy and suffering can be laughed away.[32]

While some laughter is acceptable because it reinforces and supports the desired order by (angelically) 'laughing away' evil, injustice and heresy, other laughter is more troubling and must be banished from the world because of the threat of its diabolical quality and its even more dangerous ability to infectiously involve us in its diabolism. Ingvild Gilhus's *Laughing Gods, Weeping Virgins: Laughter in the History of Religion* has charted how laughter was reabsorbed into religious culture after it came to be seen as positive and healthy by social and medical discourse.[33] This seems to be an effort to banish laughter's diabolism by bringing it into the Christian sphere and ensuring that it functions only angelically. This move, perhaps embodied in the relationship between laughter and Christianity, is by no means something only happening in this religious context. On the contrary, it seems we are living in a society that increasingly ensures that laughter functions only 'angelically'.[34]

It is my contention, then, that in a lot of cases 'comedy' has been divorced from one half of laughter's work – the demonic half. Comedy has come to be a form, even a genre, something we can oppose to tragedy, something which has characteristics we can understand and comprehend. It has, therefore, the quality of the angel's laughter, and it therefore makes sense in our social order and in relation to the total sum of knowledge in our existing world. This laughter looks down at the order below and celebrates it, taking everything lightly and repeating and re-inscribing existing structures and relationships. Even the most radical and disordering comic moments are often reduced to *making light* of things. Politics and politicians, for example, never have to respond to criticisms lobbied at them by the genre of satire or by 'comedians', as if the critique of the comedian is not serious and need not be dignified with a response. While Lipotvesky makes the jump (as most of us do) of assuming

32 Michael A. Screech, *Laughter at the Foot of the Cross* (Chicago: Chicago University Press, 2015), p. xv.
33 Ingvild Gilhus, *Laughing Gods, Weeping Virgins: Laughter in the History of Religion* (London: Routledge, 1997), pp. 13, 118.
34 Some alternate readings of 'angelic' laughter will be found in a forthcoming issue of *Critical Inquiry* dedicated to comedy.

that taking things humourously is taking things lightly, what I am after in this book is the demonic other side of laughter which is unsettling and anything but supportive of the angel's perfect order. In what follows, it is my claim that even the most angelic laughter can contain this diabolism within it, working against the idea that there are different 'types' of laughter entirely.

Laughter and indeterminacy

Theorizations which attempt to provide a 'key' to laughter or explain it in overall terms are perhaps the most dangerous (and the most common), but there is also a diametrically opposed argument which may be equally risky – the claim that laughter is indeterminate, or that it cannot be read and that the discussion ought to end there. Notions of determinacy and indeterminacy have played a prominent role in theoretical discussions of laughter. Georges Bataille's discussions of laughter take such issues as a starting point. Bataillian laughter has often been treated as a laughter which escapes rationality, and indeed he aligns laughter with what he calls 'nonknowledge', and later with 'death'.[35] This makes laughter something inarticulate, something outside language and something that definitionally escapes knowledge and understanding, making laughter something like madness in the famous discussion between Foucault and Derrida.[36] Can we speak 'for' laughter, explaining it and rationalizing it? At times in his project it seems that Bataille is clear in his answer to this question: we cannot, since laughter must always remain indeterminate. Yet, at the same time, Bataille is a theorist of laughter, returning to the topic many times in his career, showing that the effort to understand laughter must not stop. In his most important piece on comedy, 'Nonknowledge, Laughter, and Tears', Bataille writes:

> My philosophy is a philosophy of laughter. It is a philosophy founded on the experience of laughter, and it does not even claim to go further. It is

[35] On this, see Mikkel Borch-Jacobsen, 'The Laughter of Being', in *Bataille: A Critical Reader*, ed. Fred Botting and Scott Wilson (Oxford: Blackwell, 1991), pp. 146–66 (pp. 150, 159).

[36] See Michel Foucault, *The History of Madness*, ed. Jean Khalfa, trans. Jonathan Murphy and Jean Khalfa (Oxon: Routledge, 2006); Jacques Derrida, 'Cogito and the History of Madness', in *Writing and Difference*, trans. Alan Bass (London: Routledge, 2001), pp. 36–77; Michel Foucault, 'My Body, This Paper, This Fire', trans. Geoff Bennington, *Oxford Literary Review*, vol. 4, no. 1 (August 1971), pp. 9–28; Jacques Derrida, '"To Do Justice to Freud": The History of Madness in the Age of Psychoanalysis', in *Resistances of Psychoanalysis*, trans Peggy Kamuf, Pascale-Anne Brault and Michael Nass (California: Stanford University Press, 1998), pp. 70–118.

> a philosophy that doesn't concern itself with problems other than those that have been given to me in this precise experience.[37]

Calling his work a 'philosophy of laughter', Bataillie writes that his interest is in the problems that laughter raises, the issues that are broken open by experiences of laughter. The issue of indeterminacy then becomes the departure point rather than the end of the debate. To say that laughter is indeterminate is to suggest that it evades theorization, but this theorization must, nonetheless, go on. Bataille's task, not unlike mine here, is to think about the problems given rise to by the precise experience of laughter. In her book on Bataillian and Derridean laughter, Lisa Trahair writes:

> Whether we call it Bataille's challenge to Hegel or, as Derrida prefers, the 'constraint of Hegel' in Bataille's work, my interest in Bataille's writing is with the manner in which he envisages laughter undoing the tenets of metaphysical philosophy, relating concepts to their own baselessness, subjecting them to 'inner ruination', and inscribing a nonteleological method of 'backwardation' by referring the known to the unknown.[38]

This search for the 'inner ruination' within laughter, as well as the sense that laughter has the power to undo traditional philosophy, has parallels with the argument of this book. Trahair's focus is on the power that laughter has to operate against knowledge as such, following Bataille's claim that 'that which is laughable may simply be the unknowable'.[39] My theory of laughter as event in this book is attentive to this side of laughter, but has a different focus: on laughter's power to be more about the production of knowledge than about its undoing.

While there may be a radical laughter that shatters structures and tends towards disorder, often the political and social effects of laughter are found in and because of the fact that laughter is very much known and determinate. The fact is that laughter sometimes *works* because everyone involved knows exactly what it means and why it has erupted, whether consciously or unconsciously. Any laughter that is clearly directed *at* someone or something is an obvious example; it cannot play its political/social role if it is not quite clear to those laughing what it signifies (examples later). Deleuze and Guattari,

[37] Georges Bataille, 'Nonknowledge, Laughter, and Tears', in *The Unfinished System of Nonknowledge*, ed. Stuart Kendall, trans. Michelle Kendall and Stuart Kendall (Minneapolis: University of Minnesota, 2001), p. 138.

[38] Lisa Trahair, *The Comedy of Philosophy: Sense and Nonsense in Early Cinematic Slapstick* (Albany: SUNY Press, 2007), p. 18.

[39] Bataille, 'Nonknowledge, Laughter, and Tears', p. 90.

in their book on Kafka, align laughter with what they call 'deterritorialization'. Their idea of deterritorialization, developed over the two volumes of *Capitalism and Schizophrenia*, is best defined as an experience of breakdown, in which the subject is torn from the structures that construct their identity. While this might account for people seeing laughter's destructive qualities positively (those who are invested in the breakdown of structure), in fact, Deleuze and Guattari are keen to stress that deterritorialization is never separate from 'reterritorialization', the reorganization of the subject along new lines. Thus, deterritorialization can never be seen as purely liberating or freeing, and we can say the same about laughter, despite a whole history of claims that laughter liberates us (Chapter 1). At the very least, we can say that sometimes it is because laughter has a concrete and determinate effect that it functions so powerfully. When the discussion stops with laughter's deterritorializing qualities, we neglect the agenda Deleuze and Guattari set out for us and miss what laughter is simultaneously doing by way of reterritorialization – its ability to produce structures, knowledge and subjectivity in place of the ones it destroys.

The important point here is that laughter *can* be determined and determinate; it can have real effects in the world, and these can be specific and definable effects. For Bataille likewise, laughter not only throws into question who we are but also plays a role in creating who we are. Laughter has a power over us and over the things that we respond to with laughter; it can form and control both the laughing subject and the object of laughter, whatever it is that we laugh *at*. In the nineteenth century, Thomas Carlyle writes, 'how much lies in Laughter: the cipher-key, wherewith we decipher the whole man'.[40] Goethe wrote similarly that 'there is nothing in which people more betray their character than in what they find to laugh at'.[41] It is in many ways the reverse that is argued here – that laughter does not reveal what a person already is but that laughter produces characters and subject-positions and then makes it seem as though it is reflective of these already existing positions.

While acknowledging that there are as many different laughters as there are people and occasions of laughter, a theory of 'laughter as event', the main project of this book, offers a way of thinking about the causes and effects of laughter that neither reduces laughter to an overall hypothesis nor prohibits its political and cultural effects from being discussed. Ian Donaldson, in his book on comedy from Jonson to Fielding, writes that while 'comedy is a living

[40] Thomas Carlyle, *Sartor Resartus*, ed. Kerry McSweeney and Peter Sabor (Oxford: Oxford University Press, 1999), p. 26.

[41] Johann Wolfgang von Goethe, *Elective Affinities* (New York: Henry Holt, 1872), p. 184.

and evolving form always changing a shade faster than the definitions which pursue it', the idea that comedy 'cannot be profitably talked about' is equally problematic; clearly, questions of laughter teach us important realities.[42] Laughter can and must be theorized even if it can never be completely explained. Seeing laughter as event is a way to approach this difficulty. Laughter as event shows that laughter neither simply repeats and supports ideology nor shatters and liberates any essential or pre-existing subject from it. It rather shows how laughter is close to the heart of ideology; laughter repeats or rehearses aspects of ideology, but in doing so it can also reveal these mechanisms and show us how our way of thinking is put together.

Evental laughter

Perhaps surprisingly, the theory developed at the centre of this book largely revolves around the work of Hegel and the subsequent developments made on his ideas by Lacanian psychoanalysis. Gillian Rose has articulated how Hegelian philosophy can be read as a critique of the idea of ego-as-origin.[43] Following and developing this potentiality within Hegel, I offer a theory of laughter along these lines, arguing that laughter has to do with subjectivity coming into being. Psychoanalysis, which shares much with this particular reading of Hegel, is the other major theoretical model to address questions of subject construction. Lacanian psychoanalysis breaks not only from the psychiatry and psychology models which put the subject at the centre but also from the ego-psychology of psychoanalysts, including Anna Freud, who placed a focus on the strengthening of the ego. Elements of Freud's work supported this idea; the well-known quote 'where id was, ego shall be' has been read as implying that the task of analysis is to protect and defend the ego (*SE* 22: 80). Other elements of Freud's work, however, go in the opposite direction, suggesting that there is no stability or consistency in the subject. What unites a particular strand of Hegelianism with a particular strand of psychoanalysis is this interest in subjectivity coming into being. Both ask the question, how does it happen that the ego or the subject comes into being *as* original? In both cases, a part of the answer is: through laughter.

Neither Hegel nor Lacan nor Badiou, the three figures at the centre of this book, are thought of as funny or even as theorists of comedy. With all three thinkers, we might say that laughter is, at most, on the periphery of

[42] Ian Donaldson, *The World Upside-Down: Comedy from Jonson to Fielding* (Oxford: Oxford University Press, 1970), p. 1.

[43] Gillian Rose, *Hegel Contra Sociology* (London: Verso, 2009), p. 85.

their work. Each of these theorists has been thought of as, in some ways, hegemonic; all three have a drive to impose their philosophical models as ordered truths, and all three have reputations as theorists of 'structure', for which all three have been criticized. They are, partly for this reason, the perfect theorists to illustrate the peculiar relationship between laughter and order. While laughter has long been associated with disorder and breakdown, in this book I explore laughter's role in the formation of structures. In the case of each of these theorists, laughter has a ghosting presence, showing itself never to be far away even when our sense of order appears most secure.

Chapter 1 discusses a set of traditions of theorizing comedy which, although diverse in themselves, share a characteristic of connecting laughter with liberation. These arguments have often posited laughter as something shattering and destructive, either to individuals, to communities, to rules, or to structures and ideologies more abstractly. Usually such readings of laughter have been positively invested in this power that laughter may have to destroy or liberate the subject from constraining and damaging structures. The main point of this section is that laughter never only frees the existing subject but always plays a part in constructing subjectivity as well.

Opposite to these readings and arguments, laughter has been seen as different kind of reaction to already existing ideologies and structures – one which supports or reflects those structures. These discussions represent a radical break from discussions that have invested positively in laughter, but they also have limitations of their own. In the second chapter I show that, while laughter cannot be seen as purely liberating, neither can it ever be a straightforward reflection *of* or support *for* existing ways of thinking, as some readings have implied. In this I follow Julia Kristeva's assertion that 'every practice which produces something new is a practice of laughter'.[44] Laughter always involves movement and production; it always changes things. This means that even when its apparent function seems to 'support' or reinscribe an existing structure or ideology, (angelic) laughter still has the capacity to show that ideology to be unsecured and anxious, even desperate to assert itself and retain control, perhaps even dependent on laughter itself. The main point of this section is that laughter is never entirely on the side of ideology even when it might in some ways support it or impose it, because it also shows ideology to be insecure and in need of constant assertion and reassertion.

Chapter 3 is an attempt to work through the problems with these two 'types' of laughter theory (Chapters 1 and 2) by positing a theory of laughter as what philosopher and psychoanalyst Alain Badiou terms 'the event'. Seeing

[44] Julia Kristeva, *Revolution in Poetic Language*, trans. Margaret Waller (New York: Columbia University Press, 1984), p. 225.

laughter in terms of the event, I believe, offers an alternative to the shibboleths that have characterized previous discussions of laughter. The argument here seeks to avoid the major limitations with the two ideas of comedy discussed in the first two chapters. Against those who have seen it as liberating, I argue that laughter always plays a role in constructing the subject, and unlike those who have seen as simply enforcing ideology, I argue that laughter always shows that ideology is insecure. In other words, laughter shows us something about ideology – that it is unsecured and produced precisely by processes like laughter. This undermines ideology's claim to be natural and secure and thus challenges the idea of laughter as the response of pre-existing subjects to pre-existing structures. Laughter is not only the product of cultural norms but the producer of those norms, so that these norms cannot be seen as natural or secure; even when laughter is on the side of norms, it troubles them.

Finally, Chapter 4 discusses laughter and anxiety in light of these discussions, considering the fact that laughter is sometimes seen as a way of 'dealing with' anxiety. It argues that laughter can indeed be a response to anxiety, or can both follow and precede anxiety. In short, it is argued that laughter creates the appearance of order as a way of 'dealing' with anxiety by producing apparent stability, but that this order it produces is profoundly unstable and simultaneously constructs new anxieties in place of the old. The difficult relationship between laughter and anxiety, can be illuminated and discussed fruitfully in light of an argument about laughter and the event.

1

Laughter as Liberation

Every practice which produces something new is a practice of laughter.
Julia Kristeva[1]

The idea that laughter is liberating has become a 'given', since the idea is one of the most prominent arguments both in the most complex of philosophical reflections on laughter and in the most general everyday discussions of the experience of laughing. In this chapter I argue that it is not so much the case that laughter liberates the subject but that laughter plays a role in the creation of the subject that it appears to 'free' or 'liberate'.

Since 'liberating' laughter is often thought of as just one 'type' of laughter, I want to begin with the idea of dividing laughter into 'types'. John Morreall's book *Taking Laughter Seriously* (1983) and Simon Critchley's more recent *On Humour* (2002), as well as Noel Carroll's *A Very Short Introduction to Humour* (2014) have been important examples that have followed this tradition of 'typing' laughter, though there are countless examples and in fact this approach has a long history dating back as far as Hegel.[2] Most commonly there are three categories into which laughter is divided, and only one of these is the idea of laughter as liberating. However, I will show here that there are often important cross-overs between supposedly distinct types of laughter which are often ignored in discussions that follow the 'type theory' model. Ultimately my contention is that 'type theory' has worked to preserve the status or dignity of certain types of laughter (usually those thought of as liberating, harmless and 'radical') by categorizing these laughs as separable from more ideologically problematic ones. On the contrary to these tactics, I want to stress that no laugh is free of potentially dangerous political power. Jan Hokensen puts it succinctly when he writes that:

> Until 1990 most theses came down to the premise that we either laugh *at* the comic protagonist, as a deviant from social norms (thereby

1 Kristeva, *Revolution in Poetic Language*, p. 225.
2 John Morreall, *Taking Laughter Seriously* (Albany: SUNY Press, 1983); Simon Critchley, *On Humour* (London: Routledge, 2002), p. 11.

> reinforcing socio-moral values), or we laugh *with* the comic character as a heroic underdog doing battle with the social order (thereby ratifying the insurgent impulse to alter the social order).[3]

Theorists are yet to fully explore the impacts of this observation. In both cases, whether laughter reinforces or liberates from social constraints, those socio-moral norms are always seen as pre-existing the event of laughter. Laughter remains in the category of response. In making this assumption, such debates are doomed to ignore laughter's constructive and productive capacity and its key role in forming ideology. On the contrary, laughter, even when it 'liberates', can powerfully construct us as subjects, so that it is in fact the blurring of the two types that is most powerful. We might say that sometimes laughter must appear to be one thing in order to function affectively as another. As such, we need to be attentive to the potentially dangerous ideology within liberating and joyful expressions of laughter, to the 'conservatism' in apparently 'radical' laughs and to the damage that seemingly harmless laughter can do, as well as to the subversive potential within even the most ostensibly conservative laughter.

I have given this chapter a title which might itself be perceived of as adhering to a 'type' theory approach. This chapter discusses 'laughter as liberation', while the next two chapters discuss 'laughter and control' and 'laughter as event' respectively. However, whereas type theory looks to show how some laughter liberates and other laughter controls, my intention in these chapters is to assess the social and political implications of seeing laughter in these ways. I ask what political and social purposes it has served that laughter has been seen as liberating? How has our perception of its liberating qualities affected laughter's effect on us? How has the association between laughter and liberation affected the experience of laughing itself? Likewise, in the chapter discussing 'laughter as control', I ask how laughter has functioned socially, given that and because of the fact that we see it as an act of group cruelty or of social control or as the establishment and reaffirmation of established order. When it comes to my own argument that we should see laughter as event, it is likewise not a question of saying that this theory hits at the truth of laughter (as if it finally answers other less accurate discussions) but of suggesting that the framework offers a new way of talking about laughter which sees it as neither liberating or controlling. The question is not whether this theory explains how laughter works, but whether the role

3 Jan Hokensen, *The Idea of Comedy: History, Theory, Comedy* (Madison: Fairleigh Dickinson University Press, 2006), p. 24.

and functions of laughter can be changed for the better when seen in these new terms.

The first of the three apparently distinct types of laughter is what is generally called 'superiority theory' – the idea that we laugh in order to affirm our superiority over another. Such laughter is, first and foremost, cruel, and it may link laughter to sadism (more on this later). This type of laughter is almost always treated first by theorists of comedy, before discussions move to other types, perhaps showing a desire to deal with this type of comedy and set is aside, marking it off from other kinds of laughter. Thomas Hobbes's famous comments in *Leviathan* are the most famous to follow this line. For Hobbes, 'Laughter is nothing else but a sudden glory arising from some sudden conception of some eminency in ourselves, by comparison with the infirmities of others, or with our own formerly.'[4] The idea of laughter expressing superiority has a long history and by no means originates with Hobbes; Aristotle commented that 'something that excites laughter is something ugly', framing laughter as a response to the perception that the 'laugher' is better than the object of laughter.[5] Despite its ancient roots, superiority theory is by no means confined to the older history of comedy theory. Charles Gruner, for example, staunchly defends 'superiority theory' as the key to explaining 'all' humour in his relatively recent book.[6] Similarly, James English has argued that 'comic practice is always on some level or in some measure an assertion of group against group.'[7] Superiority theory remains a popular way of explaining laughter.

On the other hand, others have followed the German philosopher Theodor Lipps (1851–1914) in trying to actively recover 'the comic' from 'the feeling of superiority'.[8] In 1896 Lipps wrote:

> The comic ends in the moment when we ascend the pedestal again, i.e. where we begin to feel superior. The feeling of superiority proves to be

[4] Thomas Hobbes, *Leviathan* (Indiana: Hackett, 1994), p. 34.

[5] Aristotle, *The Basic Works of Aristotle*, ed. Richard McKeon (New York: Random House, 1941), p. 1459.

[6] See Gruner, *The Game of Humour*, p. 1. See also Charles Gruner, *Understanding Laughter: The Workings of Wit and Humour* (Chicago: Nelson-Hall, 1978). For an interesting alternative view, see Simon Dickie's recent work which troubles the opposition between care or pity and laughter, in *Cruelty and Laughter: Forgotten Comic Literature and the Unsentimental Eighteenth-Century* (Chicago: University of Chicago Press, 2011).

[7] James English, *Comic Transactions: Literature, Humour and the Politics of Community in Twentieth-Century Britain* (Ithaca: Cornell University Press, 1994), p. 9.

[8] See, for an explicit example, Suzanne Buchan, 'Theatrical Cartoon Comedy: From Animated Potmantaeu to the *Risis Purus*', in *A Companion to Film Comedy*, ed. Andrew Horton and Joanna E. Rapf (Oxford: Wiley Blackwell, 2012), pp. 521–44.

> the complete opposite of the feeling of the comic, as its classic deadly enemy. The feeling of the comic is possible to the extent that the feeling of superiority doesn't arise and cannot arise.[9]

Lipps's suggestion is that the true moment of comic laughter is far removed from anything like superiority, perhaps even diametrically opposed to it. We can estimate from this comment that Lipps prefers the idea of comedy as liberating, and indeed the rest of his discussion bears this out. For Lipps, while the comic feeling itself is liberating and equalizing, even democratic, the 'classic deadly enemy' of superiority, when we finish laughing we 'ascend the pedestal again', so that *after* laughter the structures of superiority reorder themselves and take hold once again. My suggestion in Chapter 4 is that we are sometimes dealing with the complete reverse of this: that while the actual laugh can be an expression of superior joy, we are afterwards left with an anxious residue indicating the insecurity of this superiority. For now, the point I want to make is that it is hardly possible to sustain the idea that laughter is a departure from structures of superiority when this laughter is taking place in a world which so regularly sees laughter as evidence of superiority. The ideas of 'superiority theorists' such as Aristotle, Hobbes and others are so ingrained in our unconscious (whether we have ever read these theorists or not) that we experience laughter as an expression of superiority. As a result of the fact that we see laughter as a self-affirming act that proves our superiority over the object of laughter, we experience the laughter itself as evidence of this superiority. As such, interpretations of laughter and the actual physical act of laughing are inseparable. To think of it any other way would seem particularly essentialist, as if laughter is not affected by the political and social conditions into which it erupts, as if its effects are not affected by how its social role is perceived by those involved. In short, to say that laughter is not about superiority is to ignore a powerful unconscious association between the two that influences the effects that laughter as upon us.

Opposed to this idea of laughter as an expression of superiority is the idea of laughter as release of bound or repressed energies. Superficially at least, this defines laughter as something that operates against those imposed or social structures such as hierarchy and superiority, freeing the subject from such constraints. Many have spoken about Freud and Bakhtin's distinct theorizations of laughter in this way, though their own specific comments on laughter cannot ultimately be reduced to the idea of laughter as liberating. It is worth noting that contrary to a general impression, this association between

[9] Theodor Lipps, *Komik und Humor: Eine psychologisch-asthetische* (Hamburg und Leipzig: L. Voss, 2005), p. 22.

laughter and liberation was by no means born with Freud. In the eighteenth century, for example, Anthony Ashley Cooper, the Earl of Shaftesbury, wrote, 'The natural free spirits of ingenious men, if imprisoned or controlled, will find out other ways of motion to relieve themselves in their constraint; and whether it be in burlesque, mimicry, or buffoonery, they will be glad at any rate to vent themselves, and be revenged upon their constrainers.'[10] Just as with 'superiority theory', the idea of laughter as a radical force that liberates the subject from political restraints and conditions also remains prevalent and popular today, both in academic discussions and in general discourse. Barry Sanders's *Sudden Glory: Laughter as Subversive History* is particularly indicative example, though the vast majority of discussions afford laughter at least some liberating qualities.[11] In short, the idea of laughter as release is as old and as entrenched in our unconscious as the idea of laughter as superiority. Indeed, Hobbes's definition of '*sudden* glory [my emphasis]' (the epitome of superiority theory) may itself have a hint of 'release' theory about it, which is made more of in what follows, suggesting that these types may not be as clearly separate as is often thought.

The third type of laughter which often appears in discussions of laughter 'types' is 'incongruity theory', which is rather self-explanatory: it claims that laughter arises from the perception of something odd or incongruous. I have not given this 'type' of laughter a chapter of its own in this book, since it is easy to see how this 'type' could be thought of in relation to either of the other two theories; we either laugh to affirm ourselves over the incongruous or odd (making it a self-affirming or superiority laughter) or we are forced by the incongruity to face the inadequacy of our normal order of things (making it a laughter associated with some kind of release). This third 'type' seems to have entered discussions of laughter later and has not characterized the history of theorizing laughter as the other two trends have. Another discussion which appears connected to this type of laughter is the idea of laughter as caused by 'surprise'. This idea also connects 'incongruity theory' with 'relief theory', and indeed Noël Carroll sees Freud's ideas of humour as a theory of surprise.[12] Ultimately though, it seems impossible to maintain a system of dividing laughter into types: each laugh seems to have features of more than one 'type' operating at once. The close connections between the two dominant trends in comedy theory (superiority theory and liberation theory) complicate

[10] Anthony Ashley Cooper, Earl of Shaftesbury, *Characteristicks of Men, Manners, Opinions, Times*, ed. Douglas den Uyl (Indianapolis: Liberty Fund, 2001), vol. 1, p. 71.

[11] Barry Sanders, *Sudden Glory: Laughter as Subversive History* (Boston: Beacon Press, 1996).

[12] Noël Carroll, *Comedy Incarnate: Buster Keaton, Physical Comedy and Bodily Coping* (Oxford: Blackwell, 2007), p. 27.

many of our existing assumptions about laughter. Once we throw type theory out and see that laughter can be both liberating and cruelly superior at once, things start to get interesting.

More recent work such as Simon Critchley's has moved away from a strict conception of 'types' of laughter but has at times nevertheless maintained a distinction between radical and reactionary or between liberating and ideological laughter. This move allows for positive investment in the idea of a laughter which avoids the limitations and dangers of other more 'reactionary' types of laughter such as those which simply re-enforce the social consensus or worse, assert visibly problematic ideologies, as racist and misogynistic laughter does. This risks ignoring the constructive and coercive elements that can be found in all laughter. If we consider how it is possible to 'burst' into laughter at the expense of another, or how we can laugh at another, affirming our own superiority, and then claim that we 'could not help' doing so, a language implying liberation and spontaneity, then it seems that each type of laughter contains elements of other types, meaning that 'liberating' laughter cannot be kept apart from its more cruel or ideological counterparts. In fact, sometimes we need our laughter to appear liberated and 'freeing' in order to see it as evidence of our superiority. By appearing to be a spontaneous burst coming from within, almost as if natural, laughter seems to provide evidence for the very ideological relationships established in that moment, dangerously naturalizing social constructions. If we laugh *at* another, affirming superiority, this apparently liberating *reaction* of laughter, by appearing spontaneous and unavoidable, naturalizes the superiority brought into being at the same moment.

Arguing against the assumption that laughter can be radical *as such* Andy Medhurst makes the point that laughter depends on conflict, and that a society without disharmony would be a society without laughter.[13] This disassociates laughter from 'happiness' and rather than seeing laughter as inherently liberating and positive and locates the cause of laughter in the conflict itself. This is something Mikhail Bakhtin knew when he foregrounded the problem that it is wrong to see laughter as apolitical, and that if it is overturning or disruptive, this is only so relationally; laughter's meaning is inseparable from its political context. Medhurst argues that laughter always involves change, and this is certainly true, but Bakhtin takes this further and stresses that this change is not only destructive but constructive in equal measure. Bakhtin has often served as a theorist of laughter for those seeing laughter as a positive liberating force and as such discussions of laughter in his work have often

[13] Andy Medhurst, *A National Joke: Popular Comedy and English Cultural Identities* (London: Routledge, 2007), p. 25.

missed this important dimension. Introducing his concept of the carnival, the most common way in which laughter is approached through his work, Bakhtin remarks:

> It is, first of all, a festive laughter. Therefore it is not an individual reaction to some isolated 'comic' event. Carnival laughter is the laughter of all the people. Second, it is universal in its scope; it is directed at all and everyone, including the carnival's participants. The entire world is seen in its droll aspect, in its gay relativity. Third, this laughter is ambivalent: it is gay, triumphant, and at the same time mocking, deriding. It asserts and denies, it buries and revives.[14]

Carnival laughter is destructive, although in the very act of destruction it has a creative quality that has is often less visible; carnival laughter not only denies but *asserts*; it not only buries but *revives*. This would make it closer to the earlier discussions of laughter in Deleuzian terms: laughter not only deterritorializes but reterritorializes. The carnival dissolves structure and organization, 'while carnival lasts, there is no other life outside it'.[15] It is 'the defeat of power, of earthly kings, of the earthly upper classes, of all that oppresses and restricts'.[16] Yet this does not mean that the subject is free or liberated in carnival laughter because laughter simultaneously constructs things anew. Reading Dostoevsky, Bakhtin makes the important point that carnival 'absolutizes nothing, but rather proclaims the joyful relativity of everything'.[17] This is the key point: in carnival, nothing essential or absolute is liberated or released. Instead, carnival is de-essentializing because it shows that everything is relative; neither the expressions of carnival celebration nor the cultural norms they oppose are privileged or absolute, no behaviour is free or natural. Carnival laughter undermines norms not by releasing 'true' or 'natural' unrestrained impulses but by showing that all behaviour is relative and that there is no essential or free impulse to be liberated. In other words, carnival does not believe in the existence of an essential subject to be freed. It is therefore not far removed from what Judith Butler would later call 'performativity', a behaviour which establishes the appearance of a subject

[14] Mikhail Bakhtin, *Rabelais and His World*, trans. Helene Iswolsky (Bloomington: Indiana University Press, 1984), pp. 11–12. On this, see Thomas J. Farrell (ed.), *Bakhtin and Medieval Voices* (Florida: University of Florida Press, 1995).

[15] Bakhtin, *Rabelais and His World*, p. 7.

[16] Ibid., p. 92.

[17] Mikhail Bakhtin, *Characteristics of Plot Composition in Dostoevsky's Works* in *Fyodor Dostoevsky's Crime and Punishment*, ed. Harold Bloom (New York: Infobase, 2004), pp. 33–87 (p. 36).

who exists before or underneath that behaviour.[18] If laughter is connected to liberation it is in this way; laughter has a *performative* quality in that it produces the subject who laughs. Laughter, like carnival, can produce 'free' and 'liberated' subjects, but what is freed has not previously existed waiting to be liberated but is rather forged and created in and by these moments.

What we ultimately see here is something like the production of an origin in laughter, which will be a major part of the argument put forward hereunder. Laughter can function to establish something like a natural subjectivity, or at least play a part in the production of a subject who seems to have pre-existed in order to be 'released' in laughter. This means that we need to dispel the long-standing idea that laughter is a natural characteristic of man. Laughter as release has been thought of as the human subject responding to something in its outside world, making it evidence of an essential subject who responds, but in fact the appearance of this subject can be created *by* laughter. In this sense, it would be better to say that man is the *effect* of laughter.

Reading comedy in the nineteenth century, Roger Henkle writes that we can only account for the comedy 'if we can locate the writer's position in his society and discover what he is responding to'. For Henkle, we have to see the 'shibboleths and sacred assumptions' of the writer's culture, in order to see how he challenges these in 'breaking free into art and wit'.[19] Though he thinks of laughter as nothing natural and always relative, Henkle's language of 'breaking free' implies liberation and what ultimately comes down to a belief in the primacy of a subject who exists in order to be freed. This language embodies a common problem in discussions of comedy in these terms; society is made the problem, and a subject whom we imagine to be free of social constraints in laughter is affirmed. On the contrary, we will see that laughter is more involved in constructing freedom than it is in freeing what is already there.

Ultimately it is untenable to maintain the position that there is a kind of laughter that is an inherently liberating experience. In the introduction to his casebook on comedy, D. J. Palmer notes this way in which the history of comedy theory has largely been interested in drawing out what he calls a 'safe laughter', or a laughter which can be seen as positive, as opposed to dangerous or cruel comedy.[20] In these terms, superiority theory would usually be thought of as on the side of a dangerous or cruel laughter, whereas relief theory puts laughter in the category of being positive and liberating. Palmer is right that

18 Judith Butler, *Gender Trouble* (London: Routledge, 1990), pp. 174–5.

19 Roger B. Henkle, *Comedy and Culture: England 1820–1900* (Princeton: Princeton University Press, 1980), p. 4.

20 D. J. Palmer (ed.), *Comedy: Developments in Criticism* (London: Macmillan, 1984), p. 8.

the history of comedy theory has tended to neglect this crueller laughter, often boxing it off in a short acknowledgement of 'superiority laughter', as discussed earlier. In a small section of his book entitled *Reactionary Humour*, Critchley writes, 'It is important to recognize that not all humour is [liberating], and most of the best jokes are fairly reactionary, or at best, simply serve to reinforce social consensus.' After this brief and disclaimer-like appraisal of 'bad laughter', Critchley goes on to focus his attention on a humour which can be seen as more radical.[21] If there is such a radical or subversive laughter, it is certain that most 'liberating' laughter would not fall into this category.

What is it that we 'liberate' when we laugh? In light of Bakhtinian carnival we must see that the process of liberation also produces the subject who is liberated, making it somehow constructive of identity. By some, identity itself is conceived of as the problem, a constraining force that restricts us, and laughter (Bakhtinian laughter especially) has been seen as an experience that gets us out of these restrictive confines of identity. Critchley argues that in radical laughter we are faced not with the 'affirmation of life' but with its 'dissipation' or 'flight'. For Critchley this laughter shows us how limited we are, how one is 'riveted to oneself' and this constitutes its radicalism, its capacity to 'annihilate identity'.[22] But is there really such a purely destructive laughter, with laughter only related to identity as a destruction of it? If laughter is always more than just a response to what is already there, then such an idea of laughter is insufficient. In such cases it may simply be that we are conscious of laughter as a destructive force whereas its constructive power operates on us only unconsciously.

Even if we laugh *at* ourselves, laughing *at* or even (seemingly) *in* our own destruction, we also create another position from which we laugh, as it were, *at* its former self, turning the laughing subject into an object of laughter. This process also puts the 'laugher' into a newly established position and the laughter itself acts to qualify this new position. When the 'laugher' and the object of laughter are the same thing, we could say that the subject is confronted with its schizophrenia, but this is a far less unsettling experience that one might think. Contrary to shattering identity, the subject swiftly takes up a new subject position in relation to what it laughs at. In this way, rather than showing us how limited we are, laughter moves the subject on, forming it in new ways. In laughing at oneself the subject designates how limited it

[21] Critchley, *On Humour*, p. 11.
[22] Simon Critchley, 'Comedy and Finitute', in *Ethics, Politics, Subjectivity: Essays on Derrida, Levinas and Contemporary French Thought* (London: Verso, 1999), pp. 217–38 (pp. 230, 234, 233).

was and also seems to move beyond this limitation and into a new position in relation to its formerly limited self. There is something of an establishment of chronology here in the laugh; something is destroyed and made history, and change occurs, but there is also something constructive, something is produced which can often be more subtle but can be seen as a position that is affirmed over the one that has now become history, the position of the subject prior to the laugh. Laughter may destroy structures and identities or liberate us from existing conditions, but it also creates new identities and conditions in their place, moving us on into these new relations. Here we might be close to understanding what Milan Kundera meant by 'the devil's original laughter', a destructive-constructive laugh that changes things, reorganizing subjects and objects into new formations.

This is a point made by theorist of comedy Charles Baudelaire (1821–1867). In three essays, two of which are on the subject of caricature and the other of which is called 'On the Essence of Laughter', Baudelaire makes some of the most interesting and influential comments on comedy.[23] Baudelaire writes that when we see a man fall over in the street we issue a *sudden* and *irrepressible* laugh that seems to say 'Look at me! *I* am not falling! *I* am walking upright. *I* would never be so silly as to fail to see a gap in the pavement, or a cobblestone blocking the way'.[24] Much here is shared with the language of Hobbes some hundreds of years earlier, and Baudelaire is no doubt influenced by Hobbes, but there is an added dimension coming from the humour of Baudelaire himself. Baudelaire emphasizes the 'I' precisely to show this new subject coming into being through his laughter, boasting in its new and celebrated position. Baudelaire's added emphasis makes the claim itself comic, ridiculous, and the point is that it could easily be the speaker (and 'laugher') who fell over and was laughed at. Indeed, we do laugh at ourselves when we fall over, and we laugh at ourselves for other things: things that we might previously have been guilty of before we perceived their folly and laughed at them. Laughing at ourselves teaches us an important truth that what appears to be destructive (by deriding and destroying our previous show of subjectivity, annihilating our attempts to be the sort of person who would never fall over) is constructive as well, it produces a new subject who laughs (who sees the folly of the previous one and is superior to it). The 'laughter' takes up a new position vis-à-vis its former self, the target of laughter. Baudelaire shows that the assertion of superiority is coming from nowhere; it is ludicrous or even

23 All three essays can be found in Charles Baudelaire, *The Painter of Modern Life and Other Essays* (London: Phaidon Press, 2006).

24 Charles Baudelaire, 'On the Essence of Laughter', in *The Painter of Modern Life and Other Essays* (London: Phaidon Press, 2006), pp. 147–65 (p. 152).

created by the act of laughing itself. In other words, when we read Baudelaire we laugh not only at the person who fell over but the person who was silly enough to laugh at them. Baudelaire shows us both subject positions coming into being through this moment so that laughter can create superiority rather than merely reflect it. Perhaps we can say that laughter does more than create a hierarchy. It creates a hierarchy and then makes it seem as if that relationship has always been there waiting to be perceived. In other words, laughter creates a subject which it simultaneously naturalizes. If Hobbes was consciously unaware of this, Baudelaire was certainly not.

Whether we laugh at another or at ourselves, we create two subject positions which have a particular relationship to each other. So, laughter is never only destructive – it is always formative as well. We can think of this in terms of the familiar objection 'how can *you* laugh at *me*?' which never seems to carry much weight for this very reason; it is the very fact that one person *has* laughed at another which qualifies them as being able to laugh at them. This also goes some way to explaining why laughter can and has been seen as such a powerful class tool, operating against kings, aristocrats and those in power. Since these hierarchical structures rely on ideas of natural or at least well-established superiority, laughter can be a threat since it creates entirely new hierarchical relationships, threatening to reorder the world. Though this point seems almost plainly obvious, it has not been taken up in general discussions of comedy, which have tended towards seeing comedy as an equalizing or democratizing force. On the contrary, laughter is threatening to *existing* hierarchy not because it is anti-hierarchical but because it creates new hierarchies. In other words laughter is completely anti-democratic: it always establishes structures of superiority *and* pretends to reflect them. However, because it does so it also shows them to be anchored in nothing other than material processes such as laughing, as we shall see in the discussion of the *Punch and Judy* puppet show at the end of this chapter.

This idea can be demonstrated with a famous example from medieval literature: that of Chaucer's Miller, a literary character who fits perfectly into this discussion. In the first fragment of *The Canterbury Tales*, the Miller follows the tale told by the Knight, who is of the highest class on the pilgrimage and has therefore been permitted to go first. While *The Knight's Tale* embodies class-based medieval values, the Miller's retort, told while he is 'dronk of ale', is supposed to be something of a carnival-like rejection of hierarchies and order. In this 'liberating' way, the comedy in *The Miller's Tale* has been seen as comparable to that of Greek Old Comedy. While the Old Comedy of Aristophanes was characterized by a celebration of the sexual and the erotic, of sexual 'freedom', by the time of Roman New Comedy, these characteristics begin to disappear. Leo Salingar notes that as New Comedy develops, the fantastic puns and metaphors found in Old Comedy were excised, 'together with lampooning, obscenity and exaggerated stage phalluses'.[25] The key point here is that Old Comedy, at least as it is looked back on retrospectively, seemed to embody a freedom associated with laughter and with sexuality, which has subsequently disappeared.

In brief, the comedy of *The Miller's Tale* has been seen as celebrating this freedom, the liberation of basic human impulses underlying chivalric pomp and social constructions.[26] In an embrace of natural sexuality and natural laughter, the tale has been read as embodying the link between comedy and liberation. Alenka Zupančič opposes the idea that comedy 'emphasizes our essential humanity' and counters the conception that comedy and laughter 'shows that we are *only human*', showing instead how laughter creates what we understand the 'human' to be. Contrary to our assumptions about medieval laughter, in *The Miller's Tale* laughter functions in exactly this way described by Zupančic, rather than in a liberating Old Comedy–like embrace of essential man. The Miller tells us that with the laughter of the sexually liberated Alisoun, 'she maketh Absolon hire ape/And al his ernest turneth til a jape'. The object of the joke (Absolon) is turned into an animal by the derisive and hierarchical laughter; he becomes an 'ape', the animal that most perfectly embodies the not quite human. This points us to what is most important and most complex about the role of this laughter, that the object of laughter often plays the role of ape, establishing and celebrating the human as superior in relation to it. While laughter appears to liberate natural impulses and affirm the basic human condition (the apeness of us all), it actually constructs this 'humanity' by establishing a structure of superiority over or difference from the 'ape'.

This tension and interrelation between laughter as liberating an existing subject and constructing a new subject is found in Freud's *Jokes and Their Relation to the Unconscious*. Written in 1905, the text is the foundational study for theories of the comic which have argued for almost any variation of liberation theory. Principally, Freud's treatment of laughter is indeed in line with ideas of laughter as a kind of 'release'. Freud remarks that 'civilization and higher education have a large influence in the development of repression', which means that 'primary possibilities of enjoyment … are lost to us'. Freud explains that in a joke these repressions are lifted, and the work of civilization and higher education are undone; 'we are laughing at the same thing that

25 Salingar, *Shakespeare and the Traditions of Comedy*, p. 106.
26 See, for example, J. R. Andreas, 'The Rhetoric of Chaucerian Comedy: The Aristotelian Legacy', *Comparatist*, vol. 8 (1984), pp. 56–66; David Alfred, 'The Comedy of Innocence', in *The Strumpet Muse: Art and Morals in Chaucer's Poetry* (Bloomington: Indiana University Press, 1976), pp. 90–107.

makes a peasant laugh at a coarse piece of smut' (*SE 8*: 101). In jokes we are dealing with the 'release' of more primary or instinctual impulses, which have been repressed by social and cultural norms. It is even possible to see how Freud has contributed to ideas of laughter as equalizing and democratising, since laughter operates the same on a peasant as it does on a refined bourgeois doctor. In his 2005 book *Comedy*, Andrew Stott makes this aspect of Freud's argument the dominant one, speaking of Freud as an embodiment of 'relief theory' and focussing on his indebtedness to Herbert Spencer, who provided a biological explanation for laughter as 'natural' and originating from within the human body.[27] According to Stott, Freud moves beyond Spencer's biological explanation and explains 'the need for energetic redirection as the circumvention of internal prohibitions put in place by the superego' but ultimately comes down on the same side as Spencer, asserting a concept of laughter which 'fits into an instinctual economy, a functional system that retains the equilibrium of the subject'.[28] Laughter's defensive capacity is something I explore in Chapter 4 in relation to anxiety, but the point I hope to establish here is that laughter is less about retaining the subject's equilibrium as it is about fixing the subject in a new position.

The abovementioned reading of Freud rehearses the trend of seeing laughter as having a cause located inside the individual's psychic life, and indeed Stott states that 'Freud's discussion of laughter occurs within the context of laughter as a *response* to jokes only' (my emphasis).[29] In this reading, the individual is thought of as a unified system and laughter is seen as a result of the subject's internal drives dealing with a psychological problem. In these readings of laughter as liberation, laughter is seen as merely *response*, allowing it to be evidence of the pre-existing difference between the subject and its outside world. In light of the discussion given here we might want to charge Freud with the criticism of seeing laughter as purely liberating; it is a way of affirming the existence of the ego or an essential subjectivity, ignoring the way that laughter changes subjectivity. By situating laughter as response Freud lends himself to the arguments of those interested only in why we laugh, marginalizing the 'effects' of laughter and minimizing its role in producing the very subject it appears to be the response of. However, as so often with Freud's work, other elements of his text problematize the presiding treatment of laughter as response and insist that laughter is seen not only as something *caused* but as a *cause* itself (see Chapter 2). As we see from the

[27] Herbert Spencer, 'The Physiology of Laughter', *Macmillan's Magazine*, no. 5 (March 1860), pp. 395–402.

[28] Andrew Stott, *Comedy* (New York: Routledge, 2005), pp. 138, 139.

[29] Ibid., p. 140.

following example, it is not so much that laughter liberates the subject but that it plays a role in the creation of the subject that it appears to 'free'.

Punch lines: *Punch and Judy* to *Charlie Hebdo*

Some of the best writing on comedy, including the well-known and entertaining work of Slavoj Žižek and Alenka Zupančič, has tended to use isolated examples of humour or individual jokes to illustrate points. At times I have used this method, giving brief examples and referring to various types of jokes as evidence for the points being made. Later I will show how that this slightly impartial way of discussing comedy has tended to 'eventually' or 'retroactively' turn the examples given into evidence of the points made. This might be to some extent unavoidable, since each reading of a text exercises a power over that material, but here I approach some examples in a sustained way to allow the text more space to influence the theory imposed upon it. Here and in the next three chapters, a literary example of a comic phenomenon is examined in some detail, in the hope that discussions of various forms of comedy will demonstrate the problems with existing models for explaining laughter and help to produce a new way of approaching the material. It is also my intention to analyse the laughter that occurs within the literary documents in question, to think about how these texts view the role of laughter and present it to their readers and audiences. The laughter within a text (for instance, the laughter of the characters) can often be markedly different from the laughter of the reader or viewer, and while discussions often seem to conflate the two, the connections and distinctions can be very important. Such moments can also show us the text's expectations about laughter's effects as well as the author's intentions for his or her laughter, which is particularly important given that contextual expectations about what laughter does influence the effects it has.

The first of these 'examples' is the phenomenon of *Punch and Judy*, the well-known but almost extinct puppet show. Some regional performances of the show are now all that remains of its long history. The character of Punch is a British development of the Neapolitan stock character of Pulcinella, which was first Anglicized to 'Punchinello' and eventually shortened to Punch.[30] The first record of Punch in the UK is probably the mention of the show in the diary of Samuel Pepys, in which Pepys recounts taking his wife

[30] See George Speight, *The History of the English Puppet Theatre* (London: George G. Harrap, 1955), p. 175.

to see the show in Covent Garden in May 1662.[31] In the eighteenth century *Punch's Theatre* opened at Covent Garden and by 1841 the show had given its name to Mark Lemon and Henry Mayhew's weekly magazine of humour and satire *Punch, or The London Charivari*, which was to run until 2002 in various forms. The show originally had radical roots and was perceived of as a powerful attack on bourgeois culture, but by the middle of the nineteenth century it had become a more middle class phenomenon: drawing room performances of the show had attempted to turn it into something of a moral tale for the instruction of children, and this divorced it from its working-class roots.[32] Though it was dragged on to the side of non-subversive culture, at its most radical Punch is a pre-bourgeois figure of the Italian *commedia dell' arte* recovered by eighteenth- and nineteenth-century working-class culture to challenge bourgeois life in the early nineteenth century. The show reveals the double capacity of 'laughing at' others; that it is both an assertion of superiority and reliant upon ideas of laughter as 'release' and liberation. In *Punch and Judy*, the appearance of liberation is shown to be at the heart of establishing the very structures of hierarchy themselves. Further, hierarchy is shown to be something that comes into being through laughter rather than something pre-existing that is merely reflected by laughter; laughter is shown to be the cause of hierarchy as much as it is the effect of it.

An 'official' *Punch and Judy* does not really exist: performances were always subject to the interpretation of the performer and versions were passed down from one performer to the next. Various regional versions had important differences from those performed in Covent Garden, which were themselves varied. For want of a better, the specific text used here is the one that was most widely known in the nineteenth century, the script of which was written by John Payne Collier in 1832 and was illustrated by George Cruikshank, who would soon after become one of Charles Dickens's principle illustrators. Collier's claim in the manuscript was that the script was recited to him by the travelling performer Giovanni Piccini in 1827.[33] The authenticity of the script has been questioned, but it remains the only surviving full text from which we can analyse the show in detail. It also appears at an interesting moment, on the brink of the show losing its radical edge and becoming absorbed into

31 Samuel Pepys, *The Diary of Samuel Pepys*, ed. Richard Le Gallienne (New York: Modern Library, 2003), p. 63.

32 See Rosalind Crone, 'Mr and Mrs Punch in Nineteenth-Century England', *Historical Journal*, vol. 49, no. 4 (2006), pp. 1055–82.

33 John Payne Collier, *Punch and Judy: A Short History with the Original Dialogue* (Nineola: Dover, 2006). I have used act and scene number to reference quotations from this text herein. See also Robert L. Patten, *George Cruikshanks Life, Times and Art, vol. 1* (London: Lutterworth Press, 1992), pp. 320–22.

bourgeois culture. The 1832 *Punch and Judy* show is a humorous treatment of nineteenth-century bourgeois life and its attempts to regulate and control potentially revolutionary subjects. The atmosphere of the show can be said to anticipate the 1832 reform act and the top-down regulation of behaviour that would follow it in projects such as 'rational recreation'.[34] The bill dampened a moment that E. P. Thompson called 'within an ace of a revolution' from the working class and led to an increased stress on rational amusements and local government control which the puppet show itself anticipates and tries to resist.[35]

In the script, the full title of which is *The Tragical Comedy, or Comical Tragedy, of Punch and Judy*, Mr Punch appears on screen and raises many questions about laughter and the things associated with it in an opening gambit which includes the following:

> His money he most freely spends;
> To laugh and grow fat he intends,
> With the girls he's a rogue and a rover;
> He lives, while he can, upon clover;
> When he dies – its only all over;
> And there Punch's comedy ends. (1.1)

Punch's introduction associates laughter with many kinds of freedom. He connects laughter to the idea of spending money, and to sexual freedom, as well as to the idea of 'growing fat', suggesting excess of consumption. In all accounts, regulation is rejected and various kinds of impulses are freely followed: the impulse to spend, the impulse to have sex and the impulse to eat. The inclusion of money in the list already seems to ask that we query the supposedly 'natural' status of all three 'impulses'. In any case the puppet show sets itself up as a commentary on a certain kind of laughter: the idea of laughter as liberation.

In short, the story of the show is that Punch, spurred on by the introductory resolution to liberate his impulses from any kind of repression, unleashes his violent drives onto a number of other characters, most of whom are eventually battered to their respective deaths. This idea of following impulses is presented (and has since been seen) as an attack on normative Victorian bourgeois culture, with Punch ostensibly framing himself as a radical

[34] For a major discussion of rational recreation, see Peter Bailey, *Leisure and Class in Victorian England: Rational Recreation and the Contest for Control, 1830–1885* (New York: Routledge, 2007).

[35] E. P. Thompson, *The Making of the English Working Class* (Harmondsworth: Penguin, 1968), p. 898.

who operates against the increasingly regulatory bourgeois politics of the nineteenth century, so it is no coincidence that Collier's script of *Punch and Judy* hit the press as the 1832 Reform Act was going through parliament. Punch appears to be a liberating rejection of exactly these middle class attempts to contain violent revolutionary potential in the English working class. By liberating his impulses, Punch challenges Victorian repression, or so the assumption goes. On the contrary to this reading however, the narrative of *Punch and Judy* is one that mocks the way the Victorian middle class viewed the working class, and with this, it mocks the way that we are seen as subjects whose natural impulses are violent, sexual, glutinous, and driven towards excessive expenditure. By bringing these things together in a mockery of what 'liberated desire' would look like, the show of Punch questions the idea of laughter as liberating by showing that it was not the working class but the bourgeois who wanted to see impulse as natural internal passions and laughter as a celebration or release of them. In short, far from being a comic celebration of liberation, the show is a mockery of the idea that laughter is a liberating release.

The first victims in the show are Punch's family, his baby and his wife Judy, whom he beats to death with his stick, making the family unit the initial target for an attack on bourgeois society. Punch is then visited by a number of other characters, each of whom he murders. First, Punch kills a doctor, presented as the middle class attempt to 'cure' Punch's working-class madness. The episode with the doctor has since become a comic trope and the scene has a number of reincarnations in British and American film and television:

> Doctor: Where are you hurt? Is it here? [touching his head]
> Punch: No; lower.
> Doctor: Here? [touching his breast]
> Punch: No; lower, lower.
> Doctor: Here then!? [going downwards]
> Punch: No; lower still.
> Doctor: Then, is your handsome leg broken?
> Punch: No; higher. [as the doctor leans over Punch's legs to examine them, Punch kicks him the eye] (1.3)

There is not one but three punchlines here. First, there is the trickery of Punch, and the joke is that he manages to get the doctor into the precise position from which he can aim the perfect kick into his eye. This establishes the working class Punch as smarter that the doctor who is supposed to be above him on a hierarchy of intelligence. The doctor's attempt to find the true cause of Punch's ailment leaves him vulnerable and we laugh because Punch was never really ill but looking to aim a kick at bourgeois medicine. The second punchline is the sexual joke, which recalls the previous discussion. Punch lures the doctor towards his penis, and the joke becomes funny long before the punchline of the kick when the doctor skips out the groin in his examination, moving straight to Punch's 'handsome' legs. This shows the presence of taboo, a key feature of jokes and humour and one much discussed in humour studies. One reading of the joke would be that the doctor's kick in the eye serves as punishment for his transgression of the taboo in finally reaching for Punch's groin, but this is clearly not enough. Had the doctor *not* skipped out the groin in his examination, Punch may not have delivered the kick. Instead, it is precisely because the doctor confesses to knowledge of the taboo that the action becomes unacceptable in Punch's eyes: the doctor has admitted that he is a bourgeois figure who observes taboos (Punch certainly does not), and is therefore deserving of a kick in the eye. He is not punished for failing to observe the taboo but for knowingly establishing the taboo, recognizing it and then going back across the line he himself inscribed in the act skipping out the groin area in his medical examination. The joke points to the fact that one must know and understand the taboo in order to break it. Punch has been in control throughout, setting up the episode and testing the doctor to see if he is a man who observes taboos, the opposite of Punch's characteristic liberation. Once he is proven to be such a man, he deserves his kick to the eye.

This reading also makes the third punchline visible, hinging on the doctor's use of the word 'handsome'. The word appears just after the doctor skips the groin area in his examination of Punch's body. The doctor did not find Punch's torso handsome, but once the groin area brings sexuality to mind, the leg becomes handsome, making this a Freudian slip which reveal the doctors repressed thoughts. The word handsome is a bourgeois acknowledgement of beauty, whereas the leg, which may be phallic, is sexual but certainly not 'handsome'. The taboo is created so that the doctor's act of skipping out the groin establishes heteronormativity by creating a taboo against touching the groin, but then the doctor transgresses the taboo to receive a kick in the eye. Punch becomes the judge here, perhaps operating against the homosexuality in the scene; punishing the doctor for a homosexual tendency. Punch is a homophobe, and he cements the repression involved in creating homophobia, and yet he still appears as the liberated figure in this scene. The point is that, going downwards, the skipping of the groin created the rule which the going back upwards to the groin transgressed. This third punchline is reactionary and homophobic – the actual kick in the eye which asserts Punch's violent rejection of the doctor's advance towards his 'handsome' groin. It recalls his claim to being a 'rogue' and a 'rover' with the 'ladies' from the introduction, asserting liberated desire (as Punch does) but only if this desire is masculine and heteronormative. It may suggest that he is not at all 'free' but a figure of intense repression founded on the abjection of other desires so that any appearance of them will be met with violence. Indeed, his kick to the doctor's eye may have a hint of what we could now identify as 'homosexual panic'. It may be possible to go as far as saying that the working class show mocks the fact that middle class culture believes the working class to be creatures of impulse, showing how dangerous this view can be and even showing how such a view constructs heteronormativity. Punch is not so much 'free' but is acting as a middle class viewer would expect the liberated impulses of a supposedly 'primal' working class man to look, mocking both the class stereotype and the idea of the human as invested with impulses that we should celebrate the liberation of.

After the incident with the doctor, Punch proceeds to batter to death a servant who wants to protect his gentlemen from the racket Punch is making, and then three figures of the police and legal system; a constable, an officer and a hangman, all those who enforce the rules of the bourgeois state. Each of these figures threatens to bring Punch to justice, attempting to restore order. The show's humour is derived from the continual putting off of this restoration of order, which is deferred endlessly with each of Punch's murders. The idea of laughter as a liberating departure from order is laid bare for the audience to consider. Without order and repression, the show implies, we would have not a wonderful liberated world but a world of violent misogyny and homophobia.

Punch's final victim is the devil. When he appears, after all the figures of the police state have been violently dispatched, a first-time viewer of the show assumes that Mr Punch is finally about to receive his comeuppance. At this point Punch mockingly sings:

> Jack Ketch is dead – I'm free;
> I do not care, not, if Old Nick
> Himself should come for me. (3.3)

This seems to be a comic foreboding that Punch's time is nearly up and that the devil will finally arrive to restore order, allowing the tale to become one of moral instruction which teaches children (the original audience for the show) that misdeeds will ultimately be punished. Most modern reproductions of the show end with Punch's anticipated punishment, yet in the Collier script Punch kills the devil too, figuring the devil as the ultimate expression of bourgeois ideology.

The devil is seen as one step up from the hangman, who is in turn one step up from the officer, who is one step up from the constable, and so on. The devil is a part of the police state, an agent of the bourgeois order that restricts and controls the possibility of revolution. The word diabolical etymologically means overturning or overthrowing, when in fact the devil still ultimately enforces the rule of the state (*OED*). For Punch then, the devil is not diabolical enough. On the contrary, the devil takes its place in the supposed 'natural' order or hierarchy of things. By killing the devil, Punch destroys a structure of superiority. Still, there is nothing democratizing here, since Punch simply replaces the devil at the top of the chain. If the hierarchical structure naturally and religiously existed, the devil's victory would symbolize ultimate judgment, but instead we have nothing more than the sadistic assertion of one over the other; structure is shown to be material, and imposed, rather than natural and reflected; there is nothing to stop Punch taking his place at the top of the hierarchy. The script reads, 'Be quiet, I say, you hurt me! Well, if you won't, we must try which is the best man – Punch or the Devil' (3.4). In the end, Punch comes out on top, showing us that there is nothing to guarantee the natural order of things and that new hierarchies can replace the old. Perhaps every laugh ushers in a new hierarchy.

In conclusion we can make two main points about the 1832 script of *Punch and Judy*. First, it shows that the laughter of liberated impulse and the laughter of cruel superiority can be one and the same, since Punch embodies both in equal measure. Second, it shows that new positions of hierarchy and superiority are constructed by laughter, even when that laughter might appear to be against hierarchy. Laughter is presented as something that appears to be a freeing and liberating experience, a release of 'natural' energy, but in fact there is nothing equalizing about laughter, which is shown to be an anti-democratic tool that establishes hierarchical subject positions.

Though the puppet show of Mr Punch begins to disappear after 1832, there are many afterlives of Punch in the years following the 1830s. One such is an illustration of Polichinelle, the French incarnation of Punch, drawn by famous cartoonist Honoré Daumier (1808–1879) and printed in *Le Charivari*. It shows Punch about to get his comeuppance and is accompanied by the subtitle, 'Polichinelle, Polichinelle, you have cudgelled the others long enough … now it's your turn. We'll bring you to reason.'[36] In this case Punch gets his comeuppance, so that the laws of the state are resumed, unlike in the Collier edition. A more famous and sustained resurrection of Punch is found in Charles Dickens's *The Old Curiosity Shop* (1841) via the character of Daniel

[36] Honoré Daumier, 'The New Neapolitan Buffoon'. Plate 221 from Actualités, 1855. Held at the Art Institute Chicago.

Quilp. Quilp is a direct reincarnation of Punch, similarly hunchbacked, carrying a stick with which to beat others, and Punch appears in the text to attribute the influence. Quilp is a figure of sadism: malicious, grotesque and hateful, but also strikingly humorous. Humour and sadism are linked, and in the novel Sampson Brass remarks that Quilp 'has the richest humour … the most amazing vein of comicality', and asks 'but isn't it rather *injudicious*?'[37] Humour and sadism combine in Quilp, as they do in Punch, as when he hides outside the room of his parlour, eavesdropping on his wife and her friends who think he is dead, only to comically burst in and lash out, to the horror of his tormented wife.[38] In the novel Quilp is often described as having '*burst* into a shriek of laughter [my emphasis]' while in the act of harming others.[39] The emphasis is on the spontaneity of his laughter, the way that it seems to 'release' or 'liberate' his impulses; it shows us the sadistic and even 'superior' element of a seemingly liberating spontaneous laughter. When Quilp is asked why he has been so cruel, he consistently replies, 'because I was in the humor. I am in the humor now.' This puns on the link between humour and the 'humoral theory' of the Greek physician Galen which considers feelings to be explained by internal processes, and Dickens's point is that the idea of an internal subjectivity with desires and impulses waiting to burst out becomes dangerous, justifying or even creating the desire to act with sadistic cruelty.[40] Dickens takes this straight from the character of Punch in performances like the one in Collier's script, using it as a warning that celebrating the liberation of impulses is something to be very suspicious of indeed.

In a famous essay Theodor Adorno (whose work on laughter is discussed in the conclusion) argues that Quilp, like Punch before him, 'bursts the structure of bourgeois emotions'.[41] The usual reading of this has been that Quilp blasts through the regulation of bourgeois emotions and releases or liberates drives that should be repressed according to bourgeois norms.[42] In this way, it would be a celebration of laughter as liberating, as if liberating laughter is an anti-bourgeois victory for the oppressed classes. Yet, there is more that we can add here in light of what has been discussed and ultimately it may be that the opposite is true. Quilp and Punch show that the structure

37 Charles Dickens, *The Old Curiosity Shop*, ed. Norman Page (London: Penguin, 2000), p. 462.
38 Ibid., p. 373.
39 Ibid., p. 462.
40 Ibid., p. 375.
41 Theodor Adorno, 'On Dickens's *The Old Curiosity Shop:* A Lecture', in *Notes to Literature*, ed. Rolf Tiedemann (New York: Columbia University Press, 1974), p. 172.
42 See, for example, Helen Small's association of Quilp with the 'savage' as opposed to the bourgeois in 'The Bounded Life: Adorno, Dickens, and Metaphysics', *Victorian Literature and Culture*, vol. 32, no. 2 (2004), pp. 547–63 (pp. 558–9).

Figure 1.1 Hablot 'Phiz' Browne, 1841. Reprinted in Charles Dickens, *The Old Curiosity Shop*, ed. Norman Page (London: Penguin, 2000).

of internality that bourgeois logic relies upon is something cruel and violent. Punch bursts the 'structure' of bourgeois emotions not because his true impulses are liberated but because he shows that it is false to see these drives as emanating from within the individual (and from within the working class). Instead it shows how the 'release' of energy in laughter and violence (or violent laughter) not so much affirms the power of the 'man' beneath it all but constructs the appearance of a natural subject waiting to be 'released'. By laughing along with their acts of battery and violence, Punch and Quilp construct themselves as frightening violent subjects with dangerous internal drives. As such they mock the idea of an uncivilized or unrepressed working class, and show us that laughter is not the expression of anything natural at all.

Finally, a discussion of Punch's comedy should be linked to caricature, since Punch is both caricatural and a significant influence on the future trajectory of caricature traditions. Punch's face is a caricature, with its giant red nose and exaggerated rosy cheeks, and he becomes the figurehead for *Punch* magazine because he is the embodiment of caricature. Caricature seems to be the perfect example of laughing *at* someone. It is a process that turns an individual into the object of laughter, placing them in the position from which they can be mocked and derided with laughter. While caricature has to do with a sadistic mocking and deriding of the object of laughter, laughter as liberation appears to be the opposite. As we have seen though, these two things should hardly be kept so far apart. Punch obviously recalls Aristotle's idea that laughter is excited by something ugly, and many children laugh in this way even before the show has begun, engaging in an Aristotelian celebration of themselves as superior to the ugly object in front of them. But what role does the laughter play in this process? Is laughter a response only, a reflection of an already existing difference between the person laughing and the object of laughter? Or, is laughter the process which qualifies the object as inferior or ugly compared to the 'laugher's' superior identity?

Psychoanalyst Ernst Kris remarks that 'where caricature is concerned, the belief [that the image is identical to what it represents] no longer holds good in consciousness or in the preconscious', meaning that the failure of representation to denote reality is revealed and the natural harmony of appearance is destroyed.[43] For Kris, in wit, the matter is known but the manner is secret, whereas caricature reverses this so that the manner is known but the matter is secret.[44] Caricature privileges the form, and hides the content; it challenges a structure of representation which sees the content as pre-existing and representation as the form which subsequently represents this content. Caricature, then, brings forward the question of laughing directly at something, as if it existed previously, and at the same time reveals its own part in the construction of that which it laughs at. It is, like a joke about nationality, double, since caricature implicates itself in producing an identity but, therefore, also shows that identity is unstable and shown to lack any permanent anchorage. As such identity comes into representation in a moment of anxiety. Laughing 'at' the caricature is unsettling because of what it shows us about identity: it suggests that the laughing subject is characterized by the same anxiety as the target of the laughter; the laughter of caricature asserts one over the other, but in showing that there is nothing secure behind this assertion, it unsettles the idea of identity existing prior to its representation. Adorno, in *Aesthetic Theory*, also addresses the complex relationship between caricature and content. He writes, 'Artworks are like picture puzzles in that what they hide – like Poe's letter – is visible and is, by being visible, hidden ... they are hieroglyphs for which the code has been lost,

[43] Ernst Kris, *Psychoanalytic Explorations in Art* (London: George Allen & Unwin, 1953), p. 183.

[44] Ibid., p. 176.

a loss that plays into their content.'[45] Here art creates something as hidden in being presented as visible, thus developing the suggestion in psychoanalysis. This 'hidden' thing might be thought of in terms of the original, but that original 'code has been lost' so that we are faced only with hieroglyphs, referring backwards to something we have lost, something indecipherable. It is important here that Adorno is speaking of all artwork, of representation as such. The argument I want to make is that while all representation functions in this way, it is caricature that forces the viewer to see this truth about representation. Caricature, then, can be a kind of meta-representation; it adopts other structures but shows them for what they are.

This is something that is raised in the nineteenth-century traditions of caricature discussed here. In a brilliant example of Daumier's comic caricature one can see this process very clearly. Louis Philippe's face continually signifies something other; it is not that the face simply looks like a pear, since without the middle two images the connection would be tenuous. Rather, its signification of otherness is a continuous process; one image signifies another, which signifies another, ad infinitum. The pear with which we end here bears little relation to the face with which we begin, so that caricature is not a process of embellishing an original but of effacing the concept of an original human prior to its representation. Furthermore, the pears became a regular feature of the caricatures in Charles Phillipon's publications; indeed Phillipon had drawn them before Daumier, so that they also take on an afterlife, disassociated from their own original. Needless to say, any subsequent look at the head of Louis Philippe after we have seen this caricature will imply a pear, meaning that the original is now completely lost. The later pear changes the person and then it makes the person what it now has always been, so that future changes the present rather than being a continuation of it. This kind of transformation is like the one speculated about in Thomas Bernhard's *Extinction*, where we read: 'Just think of the photo of Einstein sticking his tongue out. I cannot visualize Einstein without his tongue sticking out ... I can't think of Einstein without seeing his tongue, that cunning, malignant tongue stick out at the whole world, indeed the whole universe.'[46] Like that famous image, the first image of Louis Phillipe in the Daumier drawing is already a caricature. Caricature is not an art form that turns reality or the original into caricature, but one that shows that reality is caricatural, always eventally transforming originals into new things. Caricature then, embodies laughter's function as an 'event', recognizing the

[45] Theodor Adorno, *Aesthetic Theory*, trans. Robert Hullot-Kentor (Minneapolis: University of Minnesota Press, 1997), pp. 121, 124.

[46] Thomas Bernhard, *Extinction: A Novel* (London: Vintage, 2001), pp. 121–2.

Figure 1.2 Honoré Daumier *Les Poires* (The Pears), 1831. Published in *La Caricature*. Redrawn by Daumier for publication after Charles Phillipon's original.

power that laughter has to retroactively transform the things it responds to.[47] In this way, caricature can be the counterpart of Mr Punch. While the show of *Punch and Judy* suggests that laughter retroactively creates the *subject* who

[47] Since my later argument is so grounded in the work of Hegel I want to add a footnote here to indicate Hegel's discussions of 'picture-thinking' in the *Phenomenology*. This section of the text is not discussed in my theory of comedy below, but it would be interesting to compare Hegel's discussions of 'picture-thinking' with those of caricature here. For Hegel, 'picture-thought is the true, absolute *content*' wherein we deal with the appearance of content. Later, where 'pure insight' begins to appear, Hegel expressly says that objectivity is picture-thinking (*Phenomenology*, p. 323). This could be compared with the discussion in Chapter 3 of form and content in Hegel's philosophy.

expresses himself in laughter, caricature shows that laughter has a comparable retroactive power to transform the *object* of laughter.

One important moment which involves this power of laughter was the events surrounding *Charlie Hebdo* in January 2015. Though there is not scope here to cover the specific relationship between Islamic fundamentalism and anti-Semitism so central to the fallout, nor the question of free speech and the potential gaging of caricaturists, I want to suggest that this argument may be useful in this complex debate. This theory of laughter answers to key questions that arose in the *Hebdo* saga. First, that of why and how caricatural images could be found so deeply threatening to a particular kind of religious structure (in this case some parts of the Islamic community in France), and second, why and how the French response to the events of January 2015 included the claim that we should continue caricature and its laughter as a way of directly combatting a politics of fear and fundamentalism.

In respect of the first point, it is important to note that large sections of the Islamic community were offended by the breach of a taboo against pictorial representations of the prophet Muhammad, not only in 2015 but in earlier in 2007 when *Charlie Hebdo* first reprinted a caricature depicting Muhammad that had been originally published in a Danish satirical magazine. The *Hebdo* caricaturists, including those murdered in the 2015 attack, had expressed their surprise that caricature could pose such a threat to believers of Islam, and even published drawings depicting the idea that caricature is small compared to the might of religious belief. The caricaturist Charb, who was the principle target of the fundamentalist attack on January 7th, had earlier discussed his caricatures of fundamentalists, saying that he had difficulty believing that these images were so shocking 'that the faith of a Muslim can be shaken by a simple drawing'. Charb commented that precisely the same would ring true for a caricature of Jesus or a Catholic God.[48] Tignous, Charb's fellow caricaturist at *Charlie Hedbo*, had earlier drawn a cartoon making precisely this point, which can be seen later on.

The theory of laughter discussed here might shed light on the precise power of caricature to 'shake' religious faith. While we might define religion (very loosely) as a system that relies on the fixity of the original, seeing everything as an allegory for original truths, events and documents, the form of caricature is structurally based in a rejection of this way of seeing the world. This would make caricature a greater threat to religious essentialism than, say, the simple claim that God did not or does not exist. Contrary

[48] See the interviews shown in *Je Suis Charlie*, Daniel Leconte and Emmanuel Leconte dir. (France: Films en Stock, 2015), 1 hour 30 minutes.

Figure 1.3 Tignous, 'Allah est assez grand?' from the cover of *Marianne*, no. 925, 9 January 2015.

to Tignous's caricature and Charb's argument, the one thing that religious essentialism is not big enough to defend itself against is caricature.

This also offers a preliminary answer to why laughter (and particularly the laughter of caricature) could take a stand against fundamentalism, as some of those expressing solidarity with *Charlie Hebdo* passionately claimed after the attacks. As has been discussed, the opposition between seriousness and laughter is unsustainable. Thus, the opposition between laughter and fear proclaiming that we can fight a politics of fear with laughter (found on many protest boards at the January 15th Paris gathering in solidarity with *Charlie Hedbo*) might be missing some of the point (see Chapter 4 on laughter and anxiety for more on laughter and fear). Nevertheless, there might be another reason why *Charlie Hebdo*'s laughter could be seen as the opposite of fundamentalist terrorism, a reason that goes beyond the fact that laughter is assumed to be happy and good and fear is considered awful and evil. The previous discussion might suggest a way in which caricature could be a powerful stand against fundamentalism, offering a more precise reason why this opposition seemed such an important one to such a great many people. If caricature involves recognizing the insecurity of all representations, it might have the capacity to strike at the heart of fundamentalist views. If the *OED* can be trusted in its definition of fundamentalism as 'the strict adherence to ancient or fundamental doctrines' or the similarly strict adherence to particular tenets, for example, the 'inerrancy of Scripture' (the word is connected to Christianity slightly earlier than it is to Islam), then caricature throws this out. While fundamentalism protects the original, caricature, as I hope to have shown, effaces it. Its laughter, far from reflecting any essential identity (of the 'laugher' or the 'laughed at'), constructs us anew, creating new subjects and new objects in relation to each other. Caricature is therefore anti-essentialist.

2

Laughter and Control

The cruel joke is just as original as harmless mirth.

Walter Benjamin[1]

Contrary to the conventional readings of his work seeing laughter as liberating, Freud's argument in *Jokes and their Relation to the Unconscious* suggests that while in some ways laughter has to be seen a response (perhaps a liberating one), in other ways laughter influences how the subject is formed, suggesting it might be something of a more controlling and constituting force, something more than response. Freud wrote:

> Like wit and the comic, humor has in it a liberating element. But it has also something fine and elevating, which is lacking in the other two ways of deriving pleasure from intellectual activity. Obviously, what is fine about it is the triumph of narcissism, the ego's victorious assertion of its own invulnerability. It refuses to be hurt by the arrows of reality or to be compelled to suffer. It insists that it is impervious to wounds dealt by the outside world, in fact, that these are merely occasions for affording it pleasure. (*SE 8*: 113)

Freud separates 'humour' from 'wit' and the 'comic', accusing humour of containing something other than its liberating qualities and suggesting there is something 'elevating' and narcissistic about it. Perhaps this shows that Freud is himself a 'type' theorist and it may be that all laughter contains this quality, but what is important here is that Freud knew that there was more to laughter than purely liberating qualities. This side of Freud's discussion is rarely discussed and much more common are summary quotations such as 'as Freud argued, humor is liberating and uplifting'.[2] A more complex

1 Walter Benjamin, *The Origin of German Tragic Drama*, trans. John Osbourne (London and New York: Verso, 2009), p. 127.

2 Celestino Deleyto, 'Humor and Erotic Utopia: The Intimate Scenarios of Romantic Comedy', in *A Companion to Film Comedy*, ed. Andrew Horton and Joanna E. Rapf (Oxford: Wiley Blackwell, 2012), pp. 175–95 (p. 179).

treatment is found in Michael North's *Machine Age Comedy*, in which he writes:

> Freud seems to have made laughing as much work as remaining serious, or, to put it another way, has managed to confuse the release of energy so thoroughly with the saving of it that his humor seems to have as many constraints as the regime of seriousness itself.[3]

North picks up on an oddness in Freud and it may be that laughter pulls both ways, releasing energy (liberating) and working to rebind us (controlling) at the same time, recalling Deleuzian ideas of 'deterritorialization' and 'reterritorialization'. The focus in this chapter is this reterritorializing aspect of laughter. The previous chapter showed that apparently liberating laughter can be secretly or unconsciously controlling, while this looks at ostensibly 'controlling' laughter which produces subjectivity. Ultimately it makes a counterpart argument: just as liberating laughter is not *only* liberating, controlling laughter is not *only* and purely controlling but also contains the possibility of undoing the structures and ideologies that it imposes.

Rather than discussing the act of laughter itself, it is through jokes that Freud discusses the way that laughter can be involved in forming subjectivity. The key passage is the following:

> We speak, it is true, of 'making' a joke; but we are aware that when we do so our behavior is different from when we make a judgment or make an objection. A joke has quite outstandingly the characteristic of being a notion that has occurred to us 'involuntarily'. What happens is not that we know a moment beforehand what joke we are going to make, and that all it then needs is to be clothed in words. We have an indefinable feeling, rather, which I can best compare with an '*absence*', a sudden release of intellectual tension, and then all at once the joke is there – as a rule already clothed in words. (*SE* 8: 167)

Those who believe in a self-preserving internal subject might see laughter as emanating from within, as if instinctual. Read this way, laughter, in Freud's terms, would serve as evidence of the pre-existence of the ego, which responds to the outside world in an instinctive burst of self-preserving or self-asserting laughter. It can even be seen as a way in which we naturalize that inside/outside divide: laughter, by appearing to be the subject's instinctive

[3] Michael North, *Machine-Age Comedy* (Oxford: Oxford University Press, 2009), p. 14.

and natural reaction to certain events and objects, can make it seem as that the relationship between subject (the person laughing) and object of laughter (the person or thing laughed at) is natural. In this passage Freud relates jokes to 'objections' and 'judgments'. This is an important move because it suggests that like objections and judgments, jokes claims to perceive something about the world. At first glance, it seems that for Freud the key difference between laughter and objections/judgments is that laughter is involuntary whereas judgments are conscious and deliberately planned.

Yet, the question of involuntarity in Freud is a tricky one. Samuel Weber writes two essays which explore laughter in relation to Freud's essay, each attempting to show how complex and easily simplified Freud's initial arguments were. Weber's work reverses the idea that Freud considered involuntary laughter as evidence of the pre-existing ego and argues that Freudian laughter should not be conceived of as any kind of natural reaction. Following Freud, Weber writes:

> Laughter is dangerous to the guardians of the state, as to all good men, because of its tendency to get out of hand. This tendency, in turn, derives from the peculiar relation of laughter to the 'subject': one does not laugh the way one walks or speaks; it is not an act that the subject performs (or avoids) at will. Rather than deciding or choosing to laugh, 'one abandons oneself to'.[4]

Weber, applying the psychoanalytic ideas of retroactivity discussed earlier, shows that Freud's theory of the joke cannot be reduced to the 'release' of unconscious energy, remarking that 'just as the dream only *comes to be* in and through a process of reiteration through which it is dislocated, displaced and distorted, so the joke only *is* a joke through the effect of laughter that it produces, but which in turn constitutes it, as it were, retroactively'.[5] Thus, Freud's joke theory itself anticipates the retroactivity found in the Badiouian event. Further, since the subject does not control their laughter, it reverses the idea that laughter is an expression of internality or of the pre-existing ego. Rather, at the moment of laughter something else operates *on* the subject, taking the subject over, almost as if the subject momentarily gives up agency and submits to another power. This is a useful way of conceiving of Freud's discussion of the 'automatic' nature of the joke: the burst of laughter may be less the subject's own expression and more the subject's submission to

4 Samuel Weber, 'Laughter in the Meanwhile', *MLN*, vol. 102, no. 4, French Issue (September 1987), pp. 691–706 (p. 693).

5 Ibid.

automatic ideological processes. While the subject might be able to control the joke, laughter (which must be part of the joke in order for it to be a joke) is the excess of this control that cannot be contained. This may serve as a preliminary way of conceiving the relationship between subjective intentionality, jokes and laughter. Perhaps, rather than being the response of the pre-existing ego, laughter has to do with constituting the ego which *appears* to respond in laughter.

Earlier I defined the event, via Žižek, as 'that which exceeds its causes', and laughter may be the event of the joke which exceeds what the joke has rationally intended. Weber draws attention to Freud's comment that we find ourselves 'already laughing; our attention has been caught unawares [*überrumpelt worden*: overwhelmed]' (*SE* 8: 171). By what has the subject been overwhelmed here, in the moment of laughter? Perhaps, following Weber's implication, it is something like the invisible ideology underneath the moment at which laughter appears to spontaneously erupt. In this way laughter may 'interpellate', to borrow another term from Althusser. The 'involuntary' characteristic of laughter then, is more complex than first appears. Laughter is not the natural reaction of the ego but a moment of the ego's constitution by outside forces, the moment at which the ego lets itself be carried and constituted by other powers, a moment at which we are controlled.

In Weber's second major essay on Freud's joke book, he touches on the link between laughter and anxiety. Weber quotes Freud's claim that 'there is an intellectual function in us which demands unity, connection and intelligibility from any material'. Weber makes an important insight here, writing:

> It is inevitable that such a function will be all the more powerful during the period in which a system is in the process of constituting itself and establishing its identity, and thus imposing 'unity, connection and intelligibility' upon its material, than need be the case once the system has been erected.[6]

Laughter can be exactly such a process of imposing unity, designating subject positions, constructing egos and establishing connections between people and things. But Weber's point gives us more: while laughter can be ideology at work, organizing the world, it is likely to arise not when ideology is sure of itself and securely 'erected' but at the moments when formulations of ideology

6 Samuel Weber, 'The Divaricator: Remarks on Freud's Witz', in *Glyph: Johns Hopkins Textual Studies 1* (Maryland: Johns Hopkins University Press, 1977), pp. 1–27 (p. 4).

are coming into being and constituting themselves. This makes laughter, even when it is a powerful controlling force, a site of anxiety at which the cracks can be made visible. We might say that laughter is a highly anxious form of interpellation which occurs when the interpellating forces are weak.

This leads us to consider a number of things. First, that while 'objections' and 'judgments' seem to have varying degrees of validity, jokes, by appearing to arise 'involuntarily', seem to justify themselves and the claims they make. If laughter is a 'natural' reaction, appearing *as if* instinctually, we can hardly doubt the perception of the world it seems to assert. While we can, if we insist on doing so, legitimately read Freud as believing in the instinctual nature of laughter as response (and even of laughter as the expression of the instinctual subject), the true complexity of his discussion causes us to wonder about how jokes *appear* natural and spontaneous, making judgments and objections but also making these judgments seem anchored in nature, proven by the response of laughter. In this way laughter can be a more powerful ideological tool than objections and judgments. Second, and somewhat opposite, it suggests that this controlling force of laughter may not be as in control of the situation as it seems and might in fact designate the very fragility of the ideologies, systems and structures that it brings into being.

Rather than seeing jokes as reflective of reality, Freud seems more interested in their linguistic nature, stressing that a joke does not so much respond to something that is already there but exists only inside language. The assumption that the joke has a content which pre-exists the making of the joke is troubled when Freud remarks that it 'is not that we know a moment beforehand what joke we are going to make, and that all it then needs is to be clothed in words' but rather that 'all at once the joke is there – as a rule already clothed in words'. Completely opposed to the earlier discussion of 'laughing at' in which the joke relies on the pre-existence of some content which we consider laughable, something 'ugly' or 'inferior' which can stand as the cause of laughter, Freud posits that the joke is not a language of representation (a language which refers to something in reality). Instead, there is no 'content' to the joke, nothing which existed before the joke to *cause* or stimulate it. Freud gives examples of jokes which lack 'content':

> A borrowed a copper kettle from B and after he had returned it was sued by B because the kettle now had a big hole in it which made it unusable. His defense was: 'First, I never borrowed the kettle from B at all; secondly, the kettle had a hole in it already when I got it from him; and thirdly, I gave him back the kettle undamaged.' (*SE* 8: 62)

In the joke, each of the excuses given is valid in itself, but each one contradicts the other two. Freud explains that the key to the joke is that 'A was treating in isolation what had to be regarded as a connected whole' (*SE 8*: 62). The same process can be seen in an old Jewish joke cited by Adorno where a man catches his friend with his wife on his sofa. As the man likes both his wife and friend so much, he cannot decide which to discard, so he comes up with the plan of selling the sofa.[7] Many jokes function this way; for instance, the fake lateral thinking puzzle which answers the question 'how do you escape a room with no windows and doors and only a table inside?' with 'break the table in half, put the two halves together to make a whole, climb through the hole and escape'. Sometimes the follow on 'shout until your voice is hoarse, jump on the horse and ride away' is added to the end of the joke. In each case, the joke is that the form is correct but the content is not, the answers all work as a use of language, but do not signify reality outside of the joke. As an aside, today the funniest part of Freud's joke may be the suggestion that one might be sued for damage to a kettle, showing us how the world the joke refers to (its content) is open to change.

The point is that the unconscious will accept either or any of the answers, but the conscious demands the correct one that refers to reality conceived of outside of the joke, even if that reality is imaginary. A similar joke and a similar interpretation is offered in Mark Haddon's 2003 novel *The Curious Incident of the Dog in the Night-Time* in which the narrator, who suffers from autism and Asperger's syndrome, ruminates:

> This will not be a funny book. I cannot tell jokes because I do not understand them. Here is a joke, as an example. It is one of Father's.
>
> His face was drawn but the curtains were real.
>
> I know why this is meant to be funny. I asked. It is because *drawn* has three meanings, and they are (1) drawn with a pencil, (2) exhausted, and (3) pulled across a window, and meaning 1 refers to both the face and the curtains, meaning 2 refers only to the face, and meaning 3 refers only to the curtains.[8]

For Haddon's narrator this joke is unsettling and this is why he does not like jokes, since they unsecure his sense of ordered reality. Such jokes are against the idea that language refers to content, and instead the content of the

[7] Theodor W. Adorno, 'Trying to Understand *Endgame*', in *Notes to Literature*, ed. Rolf Tiedemann (New York: Columbia University Press, 1974), p. 135.

[8] Mark Haddon, *The Curious Incident of the Dog in the Night-Time* (London: Vintage, 2003), p. 8.

joke is an absent content or an '*absence*' of a reality behind the words. Freud uses the joke about the kettle to suggest that while judgments or objections always appear to refer to already existing realities, jokes may have a different quality. This point can be demonstrated using a well-known joke of Groucho Marx's from a famous scene in *Night at the Opera* when Chico, disguised as an aviator, worries that his words will be disbelieved and Groucho remarks 'they'll believe you when you start talking'. If Freud seems to reverse the idea of the joke relating to content to laugh *at*, instead showing how the joke can be based on the absence of content, then the Groucho Marx joke embodies the function perfectly. It shows not only that there is no content before the joke is told, but that there will appear to be content once the form is present, once the talking begins. Here, jokes make us aware of the production of content to which language appears to refer.

Jokes about nationality are a good way of demonstrating how Freud's comments relate not only to his own specific examples or to the unique genius of the Marx Brothers but to a wider functioning of jokes. Nationality jokes show the way that the joke can assert or create the appearance of presence or apparently pre-existing content. On the surface of it, the nationality joke appears to be straightforwardly directed at another group to affirm the relative superiority of one's own (making nationality jokes the perfect example of Hobbesian humour). But it seems likely that we will encounter the objection that a statement (or objection/judgment) asserting the superiority of one nationality over another is not the same as a joke which makes the same claim. This objection and insistence that jokes are different usually comes in defence of the joke; the joker can be 'only joking' and therefore 'not mean it', suggesting they are not as culpable as, for example, the serious nationalist who makes not only nationalist jokes but nationalist judgments and objections as well. The question hinges on whether the joke just reinforces an already existing ideology or whether it might do something more than this. On the one hand, it seems clear in light of our discussions that the joke could show how empty the nationalist statement is, making it (in a certain way) anti-nationalist. On the other hand, the joke quite obviously also plays a part in *creating* that nationalistic conception of otherness which it seems merely to reflect. In this way the 'joker' may be just as culpable as the speaker of a nationalist statement since both construct the appearance that what they claim is already there. Perhaps the racist joke is even more dangerous than the racist statement since by using laughter the joke can even appear to *naturalize* the identities it asserts. Freud shows us then, that the actual event of laughter is not always liberating but can also be controlling, enforcing a particular viewpoint on its subjects and naturalizing that viewpoint. While objections and judgments appear to be opinions, laughter controls by making what it perceives and the judgments it makes seem natural and uncontestable.

In *Laughter*, Parvulescu recognizes this controlling power that laughter can have and breaks from the trend of thinking about laughter as response. She comments that most of these theories 'conceive of [laughter] as a response to something else, and it is this something else that they are after – the comic, jokes, humour, the grotesque, the ridiculous, the ludicrous etc.'. Instead of this, Parvulescu is interested in what it means to be a subject of laughter, and in what effect laughter has on the individual. This is an important shift, since it begins to see laughter as productive and constitutive; laughter has to do with forming subjectivity, rather than merely being an effect of existing relationships between people and things. However, there is also a way in which the focus here differs significantly from Parvulescu's. Though she wishes 'not to divorce laughter from any potential trigger', for Parvulescu 'the question of laughter's cause or origin is [often] beside the point'.[9] In the next section a theory of 'laughter as event' is put forward, and this relationship between laughter and its causes/effects which is at the heart of it. For now though, it is laughter's vast controlling power that is important; laughter can impose an ideology and make that ideology seen natural.

Like Parvulescu, Lacanian philosopher Mladen Dolar has worked on this constitutive power that laughter can have, showing that the very appearance of laughter as something liberating can be part of the way it imposes and controls its subjects. Dolar's work on comedy has made the point that:

> Laughter is the condition of ideology. It provides us with the distance, the very space in which ideology can take its full swing. It is only with laughter that we become ideological subjects ... It is only when we laugh and breathe freely that ideology truly has a hold on us.[10]

Dolar's point is that the supposed distinction between liberation and ideology is a false one, especially when it comes to laughter; in the appearance of natural spontaneity, laughter can bind its subjects. Laughter can control and constitute the subject at the very moment when the subject feels free.[11] In short, Dolar points out that laughter can enforce the rules and norms of order rather than breaking them down, reversing the idea of laughter as liberation and also showing that the fact that laughter is perceived of as liberating is part

[9] Parvulescu, *Laughter*, pp. 3, 4.
[10] Mladen Dolar, 'Strel sredi koncerta', in *Uvod v sociologijo glasbe*, ed. Theodor Adorno (Ljubljana: DZS, 1986), p. 307.
[11] For a comparative reading, see Umberto Eco, 'The Frames of Comic "Freedom"', in *Carnival!*, ed. Thomas A. Seboek (Berlin: Mouton, 1984).

of its ideological function. When the subject feels it is naturally responding to something, that relationship between the subject and the object to which it responds itself is formed, and formed as natural, produced as something which seems to have caused the laughter and to have pre-existed it. This idea would also ask for a rereading of ideas of laughter as 'cathartic'. While laughter may have some cathartic effects (discussed in relation to anxiety in Chapter 4), we should be very suspicious of such subject-celebrating feelings of having been freed, especially those moments where we might feel more free to be 'ourselves', as catharsis implies.

The idea of laughter as imposing ideology reverses the conception that laughter is a response to failure. In his theory of comedy Elder Olson writes that:

> Tragedy endows with worth; comedy takes the worth away. Tragedy exhibits life as directed to important ends; comedy as either not directed to important ends, or unlikely to achieve them.[12]

Olson's take embodies a common position, but Dolar's argument stresses that not all comedy is failure, or that comedy perhaps always involves not only failure but success. Laughter can be ideology succeeding, it can produce something very successfully and should not be seen as necessarily destructive. Following this line, in her groundbreaking book on comedy *The Odd One In*, Alenka Zupančič remarks that 'comedy is materialistic because it sees the turning of materiality into pure spirit and of pure spirit into something material as *one and the same movement*'.[13] Thus, Zupančič reverses the traditional argument that comedy brings the ideal down to the material, or the high down to the low or that laughter brings down ideology, affirming a basic human state underneath as if it is some kind of equalizing force. On the contrary, comedy is as much about success as it is about failure; it can turn a material process (laughter) into something which seems to signify spiritual or ultimate truth (the relationships laughter responds to). In other words, the imaginary structure of superiority is nothing more than the material violence of laughter raised to a spiritual level, now appearing as if there is something behind it. Zupančič writes, 'we could say that true comedies are not so much involved in unveiling and disclosing the nudity and emptiness behind appearances as they are involved in *constructing* emptiness.[14] Laughter is not

[12] Elder Olson, *The Theory of Comedy* (Bloomington: Indiana University Press, 1968), pp. 35–6.
[13] Zupančič, *The Odd One In*, p. 47.
[14] Alenka Zupančič, *The Shortest Shadow: Nietzsche's Philosophy of the Two* (Cambridge, MA: MIT Press, 2003), p. 166.

a radical outside to ideology which brings ideology down, but instead it is *ideology at work*, creating and constructing that very appearance of substance that ideology depends upon. Zupančič's psychoanalytic point resonates with Freud's argument, discussed earlier, that jokes construct an absence that it is produced as a present and real thing by the joke. Zupančič may take the point directly from Lacan, who comments in his seventh seminar that anamorphosis has to do with 'the creation of emptiness' (*S7*: 140). Anamorphosis is an image which can only be read from a particular angle, such as the skull in Holbein's famous *The Ambassadors*. The image places the viewer in the position of searching for the truth behind appearances but the truth is an emptiness constructed by the image. The idea is comparable to Zupančič's argument about comedy, then; comedy does not reveal that there is nothing behind appearances, it does not, as Olson argues, 'take the worth away', but rather it produces the appearance of worth and truth itself: it succeeds in producing the idea that there is something, a truth, behind the laughter that is taking place.

Stand-up comedians are the form of humour which most clearly bear this out. Comedians are often praised for their insight or vision – their ability to 'say it how it is' and reveal to us a hidden or ignored truth about society. Their jokes seem to strike powerfully at what was not yet visible, making it apparent to us suddenly, much as the Daumier caricature discussed earlier seems to make it suddenly appear that Louis Philippe's face has always resembled a pear. Steve Bell's caricatures of David Cameron as a condom in *The Guardian* make it plainly obvious that Cameron's face is condom-like; and once we have seen one of these images this association will forever ring true. Yet, the perception of truth by the comedian is also constructive and transformative, changing the reality which is 'revealed' by the joke. The group eruption of laughter at such jokes establishes new relations between the laughing subjects and the objects of laughter, so that it not so much reveals already existing hidden truths but creates new ones. It may even be that there would be no resemblance between Cameron and a condom or Louis Philippe as a pear if it were not for the representations of Bell and Daumier and the laughter that accompanies these representations.

If laughter produces new truths and subject relations then we can say that laughter can be put to work for the Left or for the Right, for dominant ideology or for revolution, but that it is neither fundamentally subversive nor conservative. Rather, laughter is fundamentally ideological in that it can produce new relationships and drag its subjects into the structures it creates. Since stand-up comedians (like caricaturists) most commonly target those in power, this example seems to make the process seem ethically acceptable, but we must also be aware of the more dangerous implications of this realization. Misogynistic, racist and homophobic jokes create new truths that they appear to perceive in a comparable way to jokes directed at the high and mighty. We can even say that racism and its laughters are continually reproducing each other. However, this ideological force of laughter, its role in the production of truth, also indicates that 'controlling' laughter goes far beyond merely reproducing and reinscribing existing social relation and is in fact involved in the very production of such relations. The very fact that laughter can *create* truth in the service of ideology is also the fact that allows us to locate laughter's subversive edge.

This is because laughter not only produces but potentially *shows* something being produced. This is something that can be provisionally shown by returning to nationality jokes. The joke might reinforce a prejudice or superiority belief of one group over another, but it can also reveal that the construction of identity is based on the type of creation of otherness and the establishment of difference which is demonstrated by the joke itself. A supporting point here is the fact that in nationality jokes it is the form that is important rather than the content, so that the nationalities are interchangeable; the same jokes English people tell about Scottish people are told in Scotland about people from Aberdeen, though not in Aberdeen.[15] The joke requires a double reading; it asserts an identity, creating it, but it also shows that identity for what it is, a structure created by an assertion of one thing over another, constituting both things in the process and thereby having the potential to show that the identities or subject positions do not pre-exist. This seems to have been strangely ignored by commentators on national and racist jokes, who have even considered whether it might be racist to transcribe a racist joke when analysing it.[16] It has also been suggested that when humour becomes racist it stops being humour.[17] This may be due to a foreclosure on the idea of humour as positive and an attempt to save humour from its dangerous associations with superiority. Others have suggested that racist jokes allow racist communities to say what they really think but have repressed as a result of social sanctions.[18] Both of these points may be valid, but it is the double function of the joke which is most interesting. Something

[15] For a discussion of nationality jokes and their variations, see Delia Chiaro, *The Language of Jokes: Analysing Verbal Play* (London: Routledge, 1992), pp. 7–16.

[16] See Michael Billig, 'Humour and Hatred: The Racist Jokes of the Ku Klux Klan', *Discourse and Society*, vol. 12 (2001), pp. 267–89.

[17] Michael Billig, 'Comic Racism and Violence', in *Beyond a Joke: The Limits of Humour*, ed. Sharon Lockyer and Michael Pickering (New York: Palgrave Macmillan, 2005), pp. 25–44 (p. 25).

[18] Dennis Howitt and Kwame Owusu-Bempah, 'Race and Ethnicity in Popular Humour', in *Beyond a Joke: The Limits of Humour*, ed. Sharon Lockyer and Michael Pickering (New York: Palgrave Macmillan, 2005), pp. 45–62 (p. 48).

about laughter in a wider sense is shown to us by these jokes: that laughter both creates something and also shows (or *can* show) that process for what it is; revealing how what it creates has no basis or anchor beyond such material processes as joking and laughter. In other words, laughter's ideological function and its deconstructive quality are not separate, as 'type theory' implies, but are inseparable. The joke can powerfully impose and construct nationalisms, identities and genders – even naturalizing them – but precisely because it has this power it *can* also undo and unsecure these things by showing how contingent they are.

Lacan is the greatest influence on both Dolar and Zupančič, and it is from his discussions that these later theorists take the idea of comedy as showing something coming into being. In his eighth seminar Lacan discusses the comedy of French dramatist and poet Paul Claudel (1868–1955) and sets himself the task of getting to the heart of the nature of comedy. Lacan's theory of comedy is articulated through its connection to the object of desire and to love, a subject to which Lacan returns almost every time he mentions comedy. He writes that 'love participates in what I call the comic feeling' and that 'love is a comic sentiment' (*S10*: 243). For Lacan, love has to do with committing oneself to something, and defining oneself in relation to this object, structuring oneself around an object of desire in order to replace the more primary 'object' of desire that (in psychoanalysis) the child forgoes in the early stages of its development. In Claudel's ostensibly psychoanalytic play 'The Humiliated Father' the character of Pensée de Coûfontaine occupies the position of the desired object, pursued throughout by the desiring male Orso. Lacan asks:

> Who is Pensée in this final scene? The sublime object surely, the sublime object in so far as already we have indicated its position … as substitute for the Thing.
>
> Here we are in the presence of the object of desire. And what I want to show you … is that it is a desire which no longer has at this level of destitution anything other than castration to separate it radically from any primary desire.[19]

In Lacanian castration theory the subject gives up something in order to gain access to the symbolic order. Then (although chronology is not implied)

[19] Jacques Lacan, *Seminar 8: Transference*, lecture 19, pp. 260–338, unofficial translation by Cormac Gallagher, available at www.lacaninireland.com. For work on the connection between Lacan and Claudel, see Mohammad Kowsar, 'Lacan and Claudel: Desire and "The Hostage"', *Theatre Journal*, vol. 46, no. 1 (March 1994), pp. 79–93.

the subject replaces this primary desire which it has foregone with desire for something else. This also helps to explain another more well-known Lacanian argument, the definition of the object of desire as 'the object raised to the status of the Thing'. The concept of the Thing, later referred to as the *objet petit a* and used to describe Pensée here, cannot be achieved or even represented. Rather, it is 'the impossible' which the subject wants to reach in order to eradicate a lack which is conditional or foundational to subjectivity itself. Articulated objects of desire can therefore only be 'a substitute for the thing', which is the role played by Pensée. That Lacan should feel that Claudel captures something essential about comedy might be surprising, since there are tragic elements both to his plays and to Lacan's discussions of them. For Lacan the comedy arises when the subject is forced to give up the object to which all his attention has been attached; in this case when Orso must give up Pensée de Coûfontaine. At this point it transpires that Pensée is not what Orso had thought her to be. Instead of a pure and ideal virgin, the ultimate object of desire, she is discovered to have already been a wife to his father. For Lacan, this is the moment of comedy: the moment at which Orso is asked to give up that to which one has bound his whole identity. This is surprising because this very moment could of course be perceived as the moment of tragedy (indeed it has Oedipal echoes.) The difference between tragedy and comedy, according to Lacan, is in the relationship between the subject and its failure. He writes:

> We could even say that nowhere at any moment of these discourses is love taken so seriously, or so tragically. We are exactly at the level that we moderns impute to this love, after courtly sublimation and after what I could call the romantic misinterpretation of this sublimation, namely the narcissistic overvaluing of the subject, I mean of the subject supposed in the beloved object.[20]

The object of desire is 'narcissistically overvalued', meaning that the overvaluation of the other, rather than making the subject pale in comparison, boosts the ego of the subject (Romeo's hyperbolic praise of Rosaline and Juliet would be a case in point). As a result of this, the realization that the other is not what it was previously thought to be (Orso's realization when he learns the truth about Pensée) causes the ego of the subject to collapse.

This collapse of the subject can either be comic or tragic. The close relationship between tragedy and comedy has been commented on interestingly by René Girard, who points out that despite the disparity

[20] Lacan, *Seminar 8: Transference*, lecture 6, p. 8.

between the 'effects' of comedy and tragedy, they are structurally closely connected up until the moment which produces either tears or laughter.[21] One can respond to an event either with tears or with laughter. In the case of 'The Humiliated Father', we can (at least potentially) respond tragically, believing in Orso's true love and empathetically sharing in his grief at the circumstances that have thwarted a beautiful love that might have been. On the other hand, we can respond comically, recognizing that Orso's 'love' constructed his subjectivity and that there was nothing essential about it: that the ideals themselves are nothing more than material things raised to the status of the Thing. As a parallel we might look at the fact that the Oedipus myth has itself becoming something of a source of laughter. As a tragedy it is about a perfect and ideal love that can never be fulfilled because it crosses the ultimate uncrossable taboo. As a comedy it shows that the subject's desire is constructed by such taboos and that there is no ideal love at all. It may be that in the comic response the structuring principles of tragedy are rehearsed with a difference; their structures are revealed to us as structures and are therefore not allowed to retain their claim to significance.

The difference between comedy and tragedy then, might be that while in tragedy the existence of the ideal is allowed to continue, so that the tragic gesture is 'I am not what I thought I was'; in comedy this is reversed so that the ideal itself is reduced to nothing. In *Less Than Nothing*, Slavoj Žižek makes a distinction between Claudel and the traditional tragedies of Oedipus and Antigone, remarking that '[Pensée's] tragedy is more radical than that of either Oedipus or Antigone: when mortally wounded after taking the bullet meant for her despicable and hated husband, she refuses to confer any deeper sacrificial meaning on her suicidal intention'.[22] Using Lacan's reading of Claudel, we can add that this 'more radical tragedy' is in fact comedy. Comedy is against the idealism that Tragedy depends upon; there is no greater good to sacrifice oneself in the service of because that greater structure is also shown to have nothing behind it and to have been produced by material processes. We can now see how Lacan's theory offers an alternative to Critchley's claim that comedy shows us that 'you are not the person you would like to be'. Rather, this is the province of tragedy. Comedy, on the other hand, shows you that there is nothing beyond who you seem to be, that identity has nothing essential behind it. The comic moment shows that the subject defines itself through its attachment to the beloved object,

[21] Rene Girard, 'A Perilous Balance: A Comic Hypothesis', *MLN*, vol. 87, no. 7, Comparative Literature (December 1972), pp. 811–26 (p. 812).

[22] Slavoj Žižek, *Less Than Nothing: Hegel and the Shadow of Dialectical Materialism* (London: Verso, 2012), pp. 80–81.

but that since this object was a substitute for an earlier one, there is nothing guaranteeing or anchoring it. As a result, there is nothing behind the loss which the subject suffers. The object can be discarded without tragedy, since the ideal, perfect or complete subject has already been discarded. The final scene of Billy Wilder's *Some Like It Hot* would be a perfect illustration: when the comic subject realizes that his love object is in fact a man, the audience expects catastrophe but Osgood simply replies, 'well, nobody's perfect'.

This argument is close to a comment made by German Romantic Jean Paul (1763–1825) on the subject of comedy, to whom Lacan's discussion is likely to be indebted:

> Humor … annihilates not the individual but the finite by contrasting it with the idea. It knows no individual foolishness, no fools, but only folly and a mad world; unlike the common joker, delivering sideswipes, it does not single out a particular folly; rather it hauls down the great, but – unlike parody – in order to put it next to the small, and raises the small, but – unlike irony – in order to put it next to the great and thus annihilate both, because in the face of infinity all is equal and nothing.[23]

Jean Paul recognizes that comedy is about attacking the ideal and removing any objective validity of the ideal, showing it all to be based on nothing or at least that it is nothing permanent or secure. Jean Paul is attentive to the fact that laughter may have various effects, including those linked to parody and irony here, but it contains the potential to show 'all is equal and nothing'. His argument therefore shares much with that of Zupančič put forward 200 years later, who sees laughter as something that not only brings the great down to the small but also as something that raises the small up to the great. By doing both of these things it 'annihilates both'. In other words it returns us to carnival (discussed in Chapter 1), which affirms the 'joyful relativity' of everything, allowing nothing to retain a privileged position. Perhaps we could qualify Jean Paul's statement in this way, given what we have discussed here: comedy both annihilates and constructs, but because it reveals this process to us it allows nothing to retain hold, nothing can be seen as anchored or essential and everything is seen as *produced* and material. If laughter is controlling then it not *only* supports ideology but creates it and can therefore show it as something that is produced and therefore subject to change. If laughter has a subversive edge it may be found here: laughter, whether it works for the Left or Right, for conservation or subversion, is always materialist.

[23] Jean Paul, *Jean Paul: A Reader*, ed. Timothy J. Casey, trans. Erika Casey (London: Johns Hopkins University Press, 1992), p. 250.

Dolar nevertheless asks whether there is not still 'laughter and laughter' – two different ways in which a laugh can function.[24] Such discussions have intellectual heritage behind them. For Hegel there is a distinction between a mere 'expression of self-complacent wit' and 'the comic as such' which Hegel sees as having serious radical potential.[25] Baudelaire, despite his awareness of the cross-overs between types, develops a concept of 'the absolute comic' which is to be thought of in contrast to 'the ordinary comic' which he defines as 'a clearer language, and one easier for the man in the street to understand, and above all easier to analyse'.[26] He follows the common trend in theorizations of laughter, seeing a divide between the reactionary and the radical laugh. But something unites these two supposedly distinct forms of laughter; both presuppose a structure which the joke either destroys or supports. Ideology comes first, and the joke comes after, either re-enforcing it or challenging it.

Contrary to this way of conceiving the relationship between jokes and ideology, what we have seen in this section is that laughter is *performative* and *constructive*, forging new structures and ideologies. Laughter's 'radicalism', then, to use a term that has been tied to laughter by many of those who have discussed it, is found not in its 'liberating' or destructive power but in its *constructive* power, the very thing which also makes it dangerous and ideological. Laughter plays a part in constructing both the target of laughter and the laughing subject. Laughter's effect may sometimes support existing ways of thinking but it is also more than this; it changes the way things are and therefore shows existing ways of thinking to be insecure, contingent, material and in need of constant assertion and reassertion.

Strict jokes and pure jokes: The *Trauerspeil* of Gryphius and Shakespeare

The first chapter argued that laughter is never purely liberating or purely destructive and that it is always ideological. Its aim was to show that we should always be attentive to the constructive capacities of laughter, even when our laughter might seem to be among the most liberating or disorganized of experiences. This section explores the counterpart of this argument: that while laughter is never free of ideology, it is equally never

[24] Dolar, 'Comedy and Its Double', pp. 181–210 (p. 199).
[25] Georg Friedrich Hegel, *Aesthetics, Vol. II*, trans T. M. Knox (Oxford: Clarendon Press, 1975), p. 1200.
[26] Baudelaire, 'On the Essence of Laughter', p. 157.

just controlling and supporting of existing ideologies. Laughter always has a controlling dimension and never simply 'frees' us, but it also (because it is a moment in which we are constructed) has the potential to reveal how we are put together as subjects. Laughter plays a vital social and cultural role in forming our identities, our relations with others and our sense of who we are. Because of this, it can also be a site at which all those things are threatened.

Opposing the idea that all laughter is liberating, Walter Benjamin writes of a laughter that imposes identity. This imposition of identity, for Benjamin, is associated with cruelty and he calls it 'the strict joke'. The laughter that accompanies the strict joke is a cruel laughter which is sadistic and controlling. It is 'strict' like a stern teacher or a bound strictly like a rope, ordering the subject into certain positions and forcing them into certain roles, often powerfully and brutally and often whether they like it or not. The idea of the 'strict joke' however, goes beyond the idea that laughter is controlling. Expanding on the other power of this type of comedy, its ability to undo the very forces it imposes, Benjamin comments:

> Comedy – or more precisely: the pure joke – is the essential inner side of mourning which from time to time, like the lining of a dress at the hem or lapel, makes its presence felt. Its representative is linked to the representative of mourning ... Rarely, if ever, have speculative aesthetics considered the affinity between the strict joke and the cruel.[27]

Benjamin describes a comedy that neither does nothing other than destroy norms and conventions nor merely supports them. Instead, the 'pure joke' shows how things are put together, revealing 'the lining' of the structure, like a 'hem or lapel' on a dress. The 'pure joke' is when comedy, amidst its cruel imposition of subject positions, can momentarily and perhaps even accidentally show the lining, the seams that put us together and hold us in place. This laughter functions not to destroy, but to show the 'lining of the dress at the hem or lapel', to reveal how we are constructed even in the simultaneous act of constructing us. This idea can easily by applied to many jokes: joking can force someone into a certain position, a position of inferiority, for example, or it can be a process that mocks or undermines such hierarchies by showing them to be nothing more than the effect of a joke, something created by nothing more than a material process like joking.

In Benjamin's schema, the 'pure joke' is a development of the 'strict joke'. The strict joke is the imposition of repression and is enacted by the sadist; the enforced performance of identity is sadistic because it is imprisoning;

[27] Benjamin, *The Origin of German Tragic Drama*, pp. 125–6.

identity is imposed on the subject and makes the subject frozen and locked in identity, as Foucault would later argue without the sense of humour.[28] The strict joke is a joke that imposes identity violently onto the other, much as Mr Punch does. As this point the strict joke is on the side of ideology: it is the joke that asserts identity categories and hierarchical relationships between its subjects. However, this changes when the 'strict joke' becomes the 'pure joke'. The 'pure joke' may be read as the strict joke pushed to its extreme. The strict joke forces its subjects to perform their identity, but the pure joke forces them to continue performing it to the point where it can be seen coming into being, revealing how it is put together. The joke imposes identities but for that reason it also has the potential to show that these identities are nothing more than the effects of jokes. When the strict joke reaches its extreme moment, Benjamin writes, the pure joke makes its presence felt, 'like the lining of a dress'; one sees the construction of identity as based upon nothing, as if identity is a product like an item of clothing, sewn together and produced. The pure joke shows identity for what it is; something material elevated to the level of the symbolic or spiritual. At its most intense moment, the laughter of cruelty, which asserts identity, turns back on itself and undoes itself.

This kind of identity crisis also connects comedy to the more well-studied topic of 'mourning' in Benjamin's terminology, a connection made by Benjamin in the abovementioned quotation. The *Trauerspiel* form of mourning has been connected to allegory and to the breakdown of identity, especially by literary critic Jeremy Tambling. For Tambling, Benjaminian mourning is more like melancholia in Freud's distinction between mourning and melancholia.[29] Whereas mourning is a more normal state of 'loss' in which it is clear what has been lost, melancholia refers to an abstract breakdown in which, according to Freud, 'one cannot see clearly what it is that has been lost' (*SE 14*: 245).[30] In such a moment ideology and its rational explanations stop functioning and the world appears incoherent and lacking in meaning. Benjamin uses Albrecht Dürer's famous *Melancolia 1* to embody this loss of coherence and meaning, a failure of the narratives that make sense of the world. Benjamin suggests that the underside of comedy might have something of this melancholic quality, showing – even as it imposes and constructs ideology – that there may be nothing behind it and that narratives

[28] See Michel Foucault, *Discipline and Punish: The Birth of the Prison*, trans. Alan Sheridan (London: Penguin 1977), pp. 135–69.

[29] Jeremy Tambling, *Allegory and the Work of Melancholy: The Late Medieval and Shakespeare* (Amsterdam: Rodopi, 2004), p. 198.

[30] A connection between Benjamin and Freud on humour is suggested by Laurence Rickels in *Abberations of Mourning* (London: University of Minnesota Press, 2011), p. 173.

which provide meaning are merely temporary constructions. Freud argues that when suffering from mourning the subject turns against their own ego and denigrates it, making it the direct opposite of any 'superiority' asserting laughter. It may be that as Benjamin suggests, such ideological laughter can be pushed too far and turn back on itself, inadvertently showing itself up and hinting at the melancholia associated with the fragility of ideology.

In *The Origin of German Tragic Drama*, Benjamin discusses comedy at length and explores how comedy can both order and construct the world and reveal how that same world is ordered and constructed. Here Benjamin discusses Shakespeare, linking him to an important tradition of theatre, that of the German Baroque *Trauerspiel* plays.[31] The *Trauerspiel*, or the mourning play, is an influential form of entertainment popular throughout the seventeenth century.[32] For Benjamin the genre is not just a pocket of seventeenth-century drama but a *style*, a style which reached far beyond those plays normally considered to belong to the *Trauerspiel* genre. For example, Benjamin remarks, 'Calderon and Shakespeare created more important *Trauerspiel* than the German writers of the seventeenth century.'[33] For Benjamin the *Trauerspiel* is a form or style rather than an isolated movement, and thus it is better to speak of the *Trauerspiel* as a mode, and we can identify the *Trauerspiel* spirit in comedy that is not part of that specific German tradition. Indeed, we may encounter the *Trauerspiel* mode in modern jokes and comedy. The *Trauerspiel* mode is a form of comedy that explores issues relating to laughter's role in constructing order and social organization. It also explores how laughter can exceed the control of those employing it as a technique and threaten the very structures it supports.

A key figure in *Trauerspiel* drama is 'the intriguer', and Benjamin is keen to stress the importance of the intriguer's role in comedy. Glossing Benjamin, Samuel Weber explains that 'alongside the tyrant and martyr, is the intriguer, schemer, or perhaps better: plotter. For the plotter – *der Intrigant* – is related to the plot (*die Intrige*) not just lexically, but semantically and etymologically, as Benjamin's argument makes clear.'[34] Intrigue derives

[31] On Benjamin and *Trauerspiel*, see Terry Eagleton, *Water Benjamin, or Towards a Revolutionary Criticism* (London: Verso, 1981); Lloyd Spencer, 'Introduction to Central Park', *New German Critique*, no. 34 (Winter 1985), pp. 28–31; and Susan Buck-Morss, *The Dialectics of Seeing: Walter Benjamin and the Arcades Project* (Cambridge, MA: MIT Press, 1989).

[32] For the cultural background to seventeenth-century German literature, see Hugh Powell's introduction to Andreas Gryphius, *Carolus Stuardus*, ed. Hugh Powell (Leicester: University College Leicester Press, 1955), pp. xi–xxii.

[33] Benjamin, *The Origin of German Tragic Drama*, p. 127.

[34] Samuel Weber, *Benjamin's -Abilities* (Cambridge, MA: Harvard University Press, 2008), pp. 141–2.

from the Latin *intrigare*, meaning 'confuse' or 'confound', meaning that the word has a doubleness; the intriguer plots, drawing things together in a narrative (and perhaps this is part of his trickery) but he also confounds and confuses. Benjamin says that the intriguer has a 'demonic' quality even as it draws things together into narrative structure.[35] This 'demonic' quality is not destructive. Instead, it demonically imposes structures and order, making it comparable to Kundera's 'demonic laughter'. Benjamin also links this 'demonic' ability to construct things to comedy, remarking that the intriguer is 'in his element as the comic figure'. For Benjamin, 'with the intriguer comedy is introduced into the *Trauerspeil*'.[36] The figure of the intriguer brings comedy into the *Trauerspiel*, and the figure may be indebted to that of the Harlequin, the much more well-known stock figure of the *Commedia dell' Arte* who often plays the role of tying characters and events together and manipulating the fates of the other characters. This is a comedy about being controlled and it throws open the relationship between laughter and control.

I now turn to some examples to assess the *Trauerspiel* mode and, particularly, the figure of the intriguer within *Trauerspiel* drama that Benjamin considered so central. Following Benjamin's suggestion, the section looks for the *Trauerspiel* style and concepts of the strict and pure joke within both ostensibly *Trauerspiel* plays and within a wider history of theatre, so it uses both texts which belong to the *Trauerspiel* genre and those which do not. Here Shakespeare and Gryphius are two case studies, Gryphius embodying something of 'official' *Trauerspiel* comedy and Shakespeare showing the movement of the *Trauerspiel* style across a wider dramatic platform.[37]

One of the most important surviving *Trauerspiel* plays is German dramatist Andreas Gryphius's (1616–1664) comic rewriting of *A Midsummer Night's Dream* entitled *Absurda Comica, or, Master Peter Squentz*.[38] The play, written in 1658, offers a *Trauerspiel* rereading of Shakespearean comedy that reverses a number of traditional readings of Shakespearean comedy, in particular surrounding the relationship between Shakespearean comedy and unity. Shakespearean comedies have been read as characterized by a hidden organic unity between the characters, making everything come to its rightful

35 Benjamin, *The Origin of German Tragic Drama*, p. 97.

36 Ibid., p. 125.

37 A useful biography of Gryphius and a summary of his surviving works can be found in Matthias Konzett (ed.), *Encyclopedia of German Literature* (Chicago: Fitzroy Dearborn, 200), pp. 386–9.

38 For a transcript of the play and a discussion of Gryphius's engagement with Shakespeare, see Ernest Brennecke, *Shakespeare in Germany 1500–1700, with Translations of Five Early Plays* (Chicago: University of Chicago Press, 1964), pp. 52–104. Herein referenced by line number.

resolution at the end of each play, no matter how disruptive the temporary comic chaos may have been.[39] As Leo Salingar writes, while this kind of ending is pretty conventional in comedy, 'what is strongly or distinctively Shakespearean is the accompanying suggestion of harmonisation with the natural order'.[40] In these readings, comedy is usually seen as a liberating departure from norms, which acts as a kind of safety valve, ultimately allowing normative society to continue unharmed. On the contrary, in the *Trauerspiel* mode there is no organic natural unity but only the temporary unity stitched together and constructed by comedy.

Gryphius's *Absurda Comica, or, Master Peter Squentz* mirrors the play-within-a-play structure of *A Midsummer Night's Dream*, but whereas in *A Midsummer Night's Dream* the players intend to put on a tragedy but end up enacting a farce (making the descent into comedy accidental), in Gryphius the players set out with the express intention of performing a comedy. This comedy, as the players introduce from the very beginning, is to be a comforting one, not a radical one that overthrows established order:

> Krix: But what sort of comforting comedy shall we put on?
> Squentz: Of Pryamus and Thisbe
> Clod-Gorge: That will be most effective. It should give people fine instruction, solace, and moral lessons. The only trouble is, I don't know the story. Would it please your Highness to tell us the plot? (*AC*: 45–51)

Once the plot is explained the players confirm 'that's a comfort' (*AC*: 64). The epilogue to the performance, given by Peter Squentz, confirms the intention of the comedy, that this has been comedy applied for a purpose; 'Here ends our pretty comedy/Or you might say, our tragedy,/We've tried to comfort, warn, and teach' (*AC*: 675–8). The comedy is designed to secure existing ways of thinking, to produce feelings of security and comfort in the audience and to 'warn' and 'teach' established relationships between people and things, offering security not only to the individuals indulging in laughter but to established norms and relations.

When comedy has a purpose, and appears to be under the control of its authors and actors, its function is 'comforting', securing and re-establishing existing norms. Simon Critchley's claim that 'most of the best jokes are fairly reactionary, or at best, simply serve to reinforce social consensus' is useful here.[41]

[39] For an interesting example of this argument, see Francois Laroque, *Shakespeare's Festive World* (Cambridge: Cambridge University Press, 2003).

[40] Salingar, *Shakespeare and the Traditions of Comedy*, pp. 13–14.

[41] Critchley, *On Humour*, p. 11.

In this case it is enough to say that Peter Squentz and his performers in Gryphius's *Trauerspiel* set out to produce exactly such a comedy, a fairly reactionary attempt to simply serve and reinforce social consensus. Indeed, the play is to be performed by an apparently renowned director in front of the king and his court, setting it up as an attempt to please those in power and affirm their existing structures and hierarchies. What is more unique is the way that the drama explores the accidental or unconsciously subversive side of an attempted ideological humour.

When the players perform their 'comforting' play, the reverse of the expected happens and – like in *A Midsummer Night's Dream* – what makes the play funny is that it is not what it was intended to be. After the play the king asks 'how many sows did you commit in this tragedy?', praising the actors for the ream of hilarious mistakes they have accidentally committed in their performance (*AC*: 743). As the play has produced successful comedy in its 'failure', the king decides to pay the players 'fifteen guilders for every sow they have committed' (*AC*: 770). Squentz confirms that there has been no intentionality behind these mistakes, remarking that 'if we had known this, we would have made more sows' (*AC*: 772–3). Whereas in *A Midsummer Night's Dream* tragedy inadvertently becomes comedy, in Gryphius's text comedy inadvertently becomes comedy, so that this comedy is shown to be something that cannot be 'used' and directed, employed for the purpose it was intended for. Perhaps real comedy always has an unintentional dimension, no matter what purpose it is intended to serve. The final lines of the Gryphius play are spoken by King Theodorus: 'Enough diversion for this evening. Laughing has made us more weary than the play itself. Let the torches be lighted, and lead us to our chamber' (*AC*: 783). Comedy does the opposite to what was intended: it set out to 'comfort' and ended by making everyone 'weary'. In this sense, the sense that we attempt to completely control it, comedy is failure.

This makes the comedy of Gryphius comparable with comedy in *A Midsummer Night's Dream*, which involves something like a failure of order followed by a restorative ending where Puck famously speaks of all being 'mended'. However, a *Trauerspiel* reading of Shakespeare may see a doubleness in Shakespeare's conclusion: it may affirm a unity knowing that it does so only through the trick of plotting or intriguing. Puck challenges the audience to call him a liar: 'we will make amends ere long /else Puck a liar call' so that all it would take was a lie, intrigue or plotting, which has been Puck's role throughout, for this fabricated unity to be sustained (*MSND*, v.i, 424). However, the comedy in both plays is not entirely on the side of temporary breakdowns and failures. Comedy does not just return things to how they were after temporary departure.

Rather, the normality it seems to *return* us to is a new one. Far from having the existing orders and hierarchies simply reinforced by the comedy, the targets of laughter and the relationships between the 'laughers' and the objects of laughter are created anew. Whereas the 'skilled' director intended to direct the audience's laughter at his own targets of laughter, in the end it is his own direction and the actors who are greeted with peals of the audiences laughter as they becomes the targets of laughter. The king and the rest of the audience establish new norms by laughing at the performers and the director, just as they may be said to do in *A Midsummer Night's Dream*. In both plays norms come into being through comedy, so that it produces new relations, but these norms seem to already exist; laughter produces something which seems to have already existed. Laughter, then, is a plotting force, which is 'failure' in the player's attempt to control it but which is successful in imposing a new set of relations between its subjects. Where Puck may succeed in controlling the plot, there is no such success for any character in *Master Peter Squentz*. In addition, there may be just enough in *Peter Squentz* to make the audience wonder whether the actors in the play, and Bottom et al. in *MSND*, did not set up everything to fail deliberately from the start in the knowledge that there is nothing the bourgeois court would rather see than working class actors messing up their performance. If so, Puck becomes the butt of Bottom's joke and his restoration of bourgeois unity becomes ironic misreading.

Yet, it if is Puck who is the intriguer and not Bottom, he is crucially different from Pickleherring. Whereas Puck is a central figure in *A Midsummer Night's Dream*, looking to involve himself in the action and influence events as much as he can, Gryphius's equivalent plotter Pickleherring wants to distance himself from proceedings. From the play's opening Pickleherring wants to play as small a role as possible; 'has the lion very much to say?' he asks, and when he discovers that it is not a speaking part, 'well, then I want to be the lion', making him a mocking reversal of Shakespeare's Snug. It is the other characters who force Pickleherring to take a more central role; 'Monsieur Pickleherring must enact a principal character' (*AC*: 66–71). The premise of the play is a kind of alternate reality in which Snug plays the role of Bottom. Pickleherring, forced to play Pyramus, is the source of the 'sows' which ultimately make the performance into comedy, though they are not intentional mistakes on the part of Pickleherring, so that here unlike with Puck, the intriguer is not constructing events actively and deliberately but does so inadvertently, as if controlled from elsewhere. As if commenting on this facet of the intriguer, Benjamin says that 'the comic figure is a *raisonneur*; in reflection he appears to himself as a marionette'.[42] If Pickleherring is the

[42] Benjamin, *The Origin of German Tragic Drama*, p. 127.

intriguer then he is different to Puck in that while Puck is the figure pulling the strings, Pickleherring is pulled by them, a puppet who lets himself be controlled. This may be something of a metaphor for comedy in general: while some (Puck, for instance) try to remain in control of the humour or at least to put things back to normal if they get out of hand, others (like Pickleherring) become puppets in their own comedy.

Benjamin retains the French 'raisonneur' which the *OED* defines as 'a person who annoys by reasoning', a term which first appears in the comedy of Molière. Annoying by reasoning seems to combine both senses of the plotter or of the intriguer: it is to rationalize and make sense of, but also to be the cause of trouble or discomfort. Subsequently the term *raisonneur* has taken on the meaning of a character in a play or other work who expresses the author's message, so that the term has been appropriated by a language that upholds the agency of the author. On the contrary, appearing as a marionette is not being in the control of the author but of the plot itself, like Pickleherring rather than Puck. The figure of the intriguer, also associated with the authorial through the word raisonneur, acknowledges that he is a puppet, controlled by something outside of himself, forgoing agency over his own comedy.

Becoming like a puppet in a show in which there is no clear individual in charge of the performance shows the element of chance involved when order is produced. Laughing at this comedy creates new norms, but no one has controlled this comedy, making the new norms it establishes take the subjects involved in new and unknown directions. This imagined puppeteer is not the author or a stable organizing force but a force no one is in full control of. The famous opening of Kafka's *The Trial*, 'Someone was telling lies about Joseph K', points to exactly this function of the intriguer; the intriguer is not Kafka himself, nor the narrator, but the 'someone' who has been telling lies.[43] The 'someone' is not an individual character determining events (Puck), nor is it a controlled trajectory of events (Kafka as author). Instead it is the plot itself, which makes things happen, which is creative and which controls and dictates experience but which is not ordered from above and has a life of its own. This extra someone may be present in all experiences of laughter. Laughter may be set in motion by a set of agents with clear intentions and purposes directing their comedy and clear aims about what it should achieve (as Peter Squentz does) but there is always an invisible intriguer at work with another agenda.

The idea of a comedy bringing reality into being and playing tricks on all its subjects (even those apparently in charge of it) is powerfully demonstrated

[43] Franz Kafka, *The Trial*, trans. Idris Parry (London: Penguin, 2000), p. 1.

in Shakespeare's *Loves Labours Lost*. Costard, the young lover of the play, reveals that he fallen for the dairymaid Jaquenetta. The conversation reads:

> COSTARD: The matter is to me sir, as concerning Jaquenetta. The manner of it is, I was taken with the manner.
> BEROWNE: In what manner?
> COSTARD: In manner and form following, sir – all those three: I was seen with her 'in' the 'manor' house, sitting with her upon the 'form', and taken 'following' her into the park; which, put together, is 'in manner and form following'. Now, sir, for the 'manner' – it is the manner of a man to speak to a woman. For the 'form' – in some form. (*LLL*, I.i, 207–13)

Costard has seen the dairymaid Jaquenetta and become 'taken' with her 'manner', meaning that he has fallen in love with her. Berowne asks him to clarify 'in what manner' he was taken with her 'manner', a straightforward pun. Costard's answer is a comic exercise in the creation of narrative. In answer he states that he was taken with Jaquenetta 'in manner and form following', suggesting that her manner was the first thing which appealed to him, and following that, he became an admirer of her form. Alternatively, it could mean that he was taken by her 'manner' and that in what follows he intends to describe how he was taken by her form, or in what form he was taken by her. Though already several puns are in play, the moment is yet to become comic in the properly *Trauerspiel* mode. After this, perhaps in answer to a raised eyebrow from Berowne (as is sometimes acted), Costard makes out that 'in manner and form following' was in fact an abbreviated or condensed version of a narrative of events which occurred in reality. He jokingly makes the claim that the he was 'in' the 'manor' house while she was sitting upon the 'form', presumably an item of furniture (although the word 'form' could also refer to the act of sitting itself as it does in Ben Jonson's play *The Sad Shepherd*, a meaning retained by the *OED*). Then he 'follows' her into the park, which 'put together' is what he claims to have meant by the initial statement 'in manner and form following'.

Costard's joke shows the creation of narrative sense out of nothing but language – the words come first and then create the events that the language refers to, pointing not to the fact that comedy undermines the attempt of language to be representational but that comedy shows how language succeeds in creating a reality which it immediately appears to be representational of. This moment, then, is not a comic nonsense in which the source of humour is a breakdown of sense but rather *a comedy which shows sense coming into being based on nothing*. The laughter, like the words, produces a reality which appears to exist behind them. Even the speaker is not in charge of the reality he brings into being, since that reality later comes back to haunt him.

This comically created narrative arising out of nothing but words sets the action of the play in motion. Immediately following this scene, a letter arrives telling those on stage that the braggart Don Armado has been walking in a park where he saw Costard, 'sorting and consorting' (meaning following and then talking to) the dairymaid Jacquenetta (*LLL*, I.i, 230–66). Humorously, the event he describes is the same one which Costard describes to Berowne in the abovementioned lines, which apparently rose nonsensically out of the comment 'in manner and form following'. Thus, what initially appeared to be a joke that Costard plays on Berowne – because Berowne might have failed to understand the phrase 'in manner and form following' – turns out to create a reality on which the entire play is structured. The event it tells instigates that entire subplot of the play: Don Armado's quest for Jacquenetta and rivalry with Costard. Costard is a perfect *raisonneur* in that he 'annoys by reasoning', creating a plot from nothing but then he is subjected to the effects of that plot, as happens in the narrative of the play: he becomes a marionette. The very figure who set the plot (inadvertently) in motion becomes the party trapped within it. Making a joke, or making laughter, can be seen as a process like this. Perhaps we can say that we all become marionettes to our own laughter with no agent in complete control of the process. The *Trauerspiel* mode may be making this apparent to us.

This can be explored through the classic role of the braggadocio in comic drama. The figure of the braggadocio – of which Don Armado is a prime example – may be traced as far back as Menander, but only via Terence's play *The Eunuch*, as the Menander play from which Terence took the character is lost. There seems to be textual evidence that Plautus provided a direct inspiration for Shakespeare's braggarts, of which Don Armado is one and Falstaff is the most famous. The action of *Miles Gloriosus* takes place at Ephesus, and Falstaff's followers at the Boar's Head in *Henry IV Part 2* are described as 'Ephesians' and the host at his lodgings in *The Merry Wives* describes himself as 'Ephesian', the only two references to the location in Shakespeare (*2 Henry IV*, II.ii, 143; *Merry Wives*, IV.v, 2310). In the prologue to Terence's play *The Eunuch*, written around 161 BC, Terence writes that his play is derived from an original Menander play entitled *The Flatterer*, in which 'there are a sponger who flatters and a soldier who boasts'.[44] Menander died around 291 BC. Earlier still, the character is likely to be a derivation of the *alazôn*, an impostor who thinks of himself as greater than he is.[45]

[44] Terence, *The Comedies*, ed. and trans. Betty Radice (London: Penguin, 1976), p. 166.

[45] This link is well established by Northrop Frye in *The Anatomy of Criticism* (Princeton: Princeton University Press, 1957), p. 172.

The *alazôn* is a typical figure in Greek Old Comedy, found notably in *Aristophanes*.[46]

Frye summarizes the central movement in Old Comedy as 'the movement from *pistis* to *gnosis*, from a society controlled by habit, ritual bondage, arbitrary law and the older characters to a society controlled by youth and pragmatic freedom'. Relating it to wider comic theory, Frye argues that such a development is a movement from illusion to reality when 'illusion is whatever is fixed or definable, and reality is best understood as its negation'.[47] In keeping with this model, in Aristophanes's *Lysistrata*, the 'chorus of old men' who control society are thwarted by the Athenian women, who refuse the men sexual pleasure until they have agreed to stop the interminable Peloponnesian war.[48] Eventually the men relent and the sexes make peace amid a show of exaggerated erect phalli comically produced by the sexual deprivation. The play is overtly sexual and comes to an excessive carnivalesque conclusion. In short, laughter is presented as liberating and carnival insofar as carnival 'means the defeat of power, of earthly kings, of the earthly upper classes, of all that oppresses and restricts'.[49] Bahktin indeed briefly notes a sense of carnival in Aristophanes, and such a description would fit Frye's definition of Old Comedy.[50] In *Lysitstrata* the carnival atmosphere is at its most intense at the conclusion of the play. This movement is opposed that of Shakespearean comedy in which any carnival atmosphere, bawdy festivity and gender subversion is reconciled at the plays conclusion, with life returning to organized structure. In *As You Like It*, for example, the illusion is the muddled state of relations in which Oliver is in love with Celia's false identity and she and Rosalind are dressed as men. As discussed earlier, Puck plays this role in *A Midsummer Night's Dream*. The conclusion of each play returns the characters to normal monogamous patriarchal marriages, which represents a return to reality after temporary forays into fantasy. While in Shakespeare reality is order and chaos is illusion, in Old Comedy the categories are reversed so that reality is chaos and illusion is order.

If Greek Old Comedy presents laughter as liberation, Roman New Comedy presents laughter as control. The laughter of New Comedy is based on mocking, tricking, humiliating and embarrassing. It is a laughter

46 A*lazôn* was also the title of a Greek play from which Plautus says he took his *Miles Gloriosus*.

47 Frye, *The Anatomy of Criticism*, p. 172.

48 Aristophanes, *Lysistrata and Other Plays*, ed. and trans. Alan H. Sommerstein (London: Penguin, 2002).

49 Bakhtin, *Rabelais and His World*, p. 92.

50 Ibid., p. 98.

directed *at* an individual, not a laughter that subsumes the stage, engulfing all in a heterogeneous chaos. Such a comedy is interested in an inverse function of laughter compared with Old Comedy; a laughter than functions not to dissolve existing ways of thinking but rather to reinforce existing value systems, a laughter which produces order rather than breaking it down. Plautus's *Miles Gloriosus*, for example, is dominated by a Hobbesian laughter in which one laughs to confirm one's own distance from the subject of the jokes. In Terence's *The Eunuch*, the braggart Thraso is not made aware of himself as the subject of mockery at all. The play concludes with the soldier still convinced of his own glorious nature, the flatterer humorously remarking that he 'only had to reveal [Thraso's] true character and praise [him] according to [his] merits' in order to get him accepted back into society.[51] The implication of this is that it hardly matters whether we are subject or object of laughter. In Plautus, however, the braggadocio Pyrgopolynices is made the subject of everyone else's trickery and at the play's conclusion he realizes he has been tricked and is subjected to harsh mocking laughter. In the moment he is utterly humiliated and it is only by laughing at himself that he is able to integrate back into society by accepting the new subject position he has been forced into by the peals of laughter directed at him.

To conclude, Old Comedy presents old laughter: that which is thought of as freeing and liberating, with its associations of buffoonery and mirth. This has been discussed in Chapter 1, with all its dangers and limitations. With New Comedy we see the development of what Benjamin's calls the 'strict joke', a laughter that is directed at an individual and which involved forcing identity cruelly onto the subjects of laughter. This is a laughter of control, which has been the subject of this chapter. This 'laughter as control' is a laughter that reinforces and reiterates existing subject positions and existing ideologies, serving to entrench ideology further still. Yet, with the *Trauerspiel* we also see the 'strict' joke turn into the 'pure' one. This is when, to paraphrase Benjamin, our strict joke and its attempt to impose identity is pushed so far that it begins to reveal this identity structure to us, showing us how we are put together as subjects.

The figure of the braggart is an interesting one because it travels through all three of these modes of comedy, the Old, the New and the *Trauerspiel*. We might say that the braggart travels through comedy as liberating (Old Comedy), comedy as control (New Comedy) and comedy as exceeding control (*Trauerspiel*) Perhaps the most famous quotation from the most

[51] Terence, *The Comedies*, ed. and trans. Betty Radice (London: Penguin, 1976).

famous braggart of all time encapsulates what the figure of the braggart becomes in the *Trauerspiel* mode. Sir John Falstaff remarks:

> Man, is not able to invent anything that tends to laughter more than I invent or is invented on me: I am not only witty in myself, but the cause that wit is in others.
>
> (*2 Henry IV*, I.ii, 8–12.5)

Falstaff knows that laughter's effects are not entirely consciously deployed, often producing unknown futures and ideologies, and that sometimes we are subjected to the effects of laughter with no agency in the matter: we do not just 'invent' laughter, it is 'invented *on* us', as if it has an 'intriguing' power of its own. Falstaff also knows that laughter is not just a response but a cause; it is not only that he is the cause of wit in others (making a laughter response, to Falstaff and his jokes, for example) but the cause 'that wit is', making laughter something productive and constitutive even though he cannot control its effects as author or comedian. Laughter itself plots, like a conspirator or an intriguer, turning its subjects into marionettes, puppets guided from outside. Laughter *shows* ideology being imposed, and this can make laughter threatening and dangerous to that very ideology. Althusser commented that 'ideology never says "I am ideological"', but laughter sometimes does.[52]

The first chapter argued that laughter is not as liberating as it seems, and is involved in controlling and coercing its subjects. This second chapter has argued that if laughter is ideological and productive then it also has the capacity *to show things being produced*. It is here that its radical edge is found; laughter may be coercive and controlling, but it also has the capacity to show us the structures that it supports *coming into being* and to reveal how they are put together. In this way, there can be a subversive underside in even the most ideological laughter. The next chapter will develop these observations into a theory of laughter.

[52] Louis Althusser, *Lenin and Philosophy and Other Essays*, trans. Ben Brewster. (New York: Monthly Review Press, 2001), p. 118.

3

Laughter as Event

The origin is laughing.

Jean-Luc Nancy[1]

As discussed in the first chapter, discussions of *why* we laugh have seen laughter purely as an *effect* of something else and have therefore tended to neglect the constitutive and productive powers that laughter can have. On the other hand, the second chapter discussed writers such as Anca Parvuescu, Mladen Dolar and Alenka Zupančič, who have analysed the formative *effects* of laughter, exploring the various impacts that laughter has on the subject in relation to ideology. In doing so, these discussions have radically transformed studies of comedy. Yet, in placing the focus on the effects of laughter, these discussions have sometimes been inclined to divorce laughter from the things that provoke and stimulate it. Indeed, for Parvulescu, 'the question of laughter's cause or origin is [often] beside the point'.[2]

In leaving the discussion of causes behind there is a danger of neglecting the close relationship between laughter and the objects we laugh at or the events that make us laugh. It is fair to say that, at least almost always, we seem to be laughing at or because of something, and it may be that laughter is never *without an object* (this argument is picked up in Chapter 4). While laughter 'produces something new' (see Chapter 1) and cannot be reduced to a response to a set of already existing conditions, laughter's cause never seems to be 'beside the point'. This chapter is about the relationship between the trigger, cause or object of laughter, and the event of the laugh itself. The first argument of the chapter is that the two dominant ways of thinking about laughter, either as liberating or as controlling, can be negotiated by a third hypothesis, the idea that laughter should be seen as what Alain Badiou terms 'the event'. This allows us to see that laughter must always be treated in relation to the objects or subjects that stimulate it, meaning that there is no

1 Jean-Luc Nancy, 'Elliptical Sense', *Research in Phenomenology*, vol. 18 (1988), pp. 175–91.
2 Parvulescu, *Laughter*, pp. 3, 4.

apolitical or ahistorical laughter, no laughter without a cause. It also allows us to see that laughter is never merely an effect of a pre-existing cause but instead has a power to modify and change the very things which cause it. In other words, laughter changes the political and historical situations that it arises in and also plays a kind of trick which makes it seem as if it has been merely an *effect* of this apparently already existing situation.

As suggested earlier, seeing laughter as event means recognizing that part of laughter's *effect* is the power to retroactively change its *causes*. The effect of laughter modifies the thing laughed at (the object of laughter) and it modifies the person laughing (the subject of laughter). An example would be to show the role of jokes in constructing national identities, rather than seeing a joke as something that merely reinforces existing nationalisms. These jokes, while routed in ideology, also exceed and change it. Žižek defines the event as 'the effect that seems to exceed its causes'.[3] An event is that which exceeds its causes, so that while it has political stimuli, it also establishes new causes for itself, its effects retroactively restructuring the past into a new structure and bringing us within this reordered world, whether we like it or not. In other words, laughter brings the subjects involved (those telling the jokes, those laughing, and those targeted) into new ideological structures which are produced, entrenched, naturalized and enforced by the process of laughter. This means that laughter can be radical, conservative, ideological or liberating, depending on the structures it responds to and reconstructs. It also means that laughter always contains the possibility to unsecure, showing us how precarious our subjectivity is. Morreal's influential book *Taking Laughter Seriously* treats the various 'types' of laughter before proposing a theory of its own, claiming that laughter involves 'a pleasant psychological shift'. Commenting on Morreal, Jacques Le Gof points out that we run into a problem when we consider how we might define this 'shift'?[4] A different argument from Morreall, but one which tries to take his idea further, this section looks to explore the mechanism behind laughter's transformative quality, offering a framework for how we might begin to talk about the 'shifts' that occur in laughter.

The second project of the chapter is to trace the conceptualization of the 'event' through its history in psychoanalysis and Hegelianism, showing that while the philosophical concept of the event has not been directly connected to comedy by any of the principle philosophers to develop the idea, laughter has never been far away. Laughter ghosts the work of Hegel, Freud, Lacan and

[3] Žižek, *Event*, p. 3.

[4] Jacques Le Gof, 'Laughter in the Middle Ages', in *A Cultural History of Humour*, ed. Jan Bremmer and Herman Roodenburg (Oxford: Polity, 1997), pp. 40–53 (p. 47).

Badiou as the concept of the event comes into being, and this chapter picks up on this key link and then reads laughter back in light of the connection. Before discussing Badiou, the chapter works through an analysis of Hegel's ideas of 'beginning' and *Aufhebung*, then moves to a psychoanalytic discussion of 'retroactivity', both of which are key conceptual developments in the development of what Badiou would call 'the event'. All these parts of the chain that led to Badiou's final formulation of the concept in *Being and Event* indicate a relationship between the event and laughter which has never been explored.

This may be because the idea of laughter as event is not something that Alain Badiou himself would agree with, and this book is not a straightforward application of Badiou in a new context. To see laughter as an event is to read Badiou somewhat against the grain. For Badiou, there are four kinds of 'event' and laughter is not one of them. A Badiouian event is a very rare and unusual occurrence, something that occasionally interrupts the trajectory of things and reorders the world around it. Arguing that laughter is an event means seeing this process as something that happens a great many times each day to a great many people and in a great many different ways. The book therefore involves rethinking the event itself, a topic that has received renewed attention in philosophy and critical studies over the past few years. In this regard it may be that a different model of subjectivity is implied than the one which Badiou himself works from, focussing on the construction of the subject by gradual increments (something we could call mini-events) rather that the formation and defection of subjectivity in terms of major eventual shifts.

Beginnings: Hegel the comedian

Writing in *Flüchtlingsgespräche*, Bertolt Brecht says that Hegel had what it takes to be one of the greatest comedians, and that his comedy ought to be thought of as destructive and disordering. Brecht's comments therefore work in opposition to a whole history of philosophy that has asserted Hegel's status as the philosopher of complete and secure totality. They also contradict the general idea that Hegel's philosophy could not be more serious and less comic and playful. Typically, Hegel would be one of the last philosophers to be associated with anxiety, disorder or comedy and yet Brecht sees his philosophy as embodying all of these things, writing:

> [Hegel] had what it takes to be one of the greatest comedians among philosophers, comparable only to Socrates, who had a similar method… He had a twitch of the eye, as far as I can see, with which he was born,

> like a birth defect and which he kept until his death, without him ever becoming conscious of it. He was always winking in the same way that others had an unsuppressable St. Vitus' dance. His sense of humor was such that he could not think, for example, of order without disorder. It was clear to him that in the immediate proximity of the greatest order, there was to be found the greatest disorder, and he even went so far as saying: in one and the same place![5]

Brecht refers to the St Vitus dance, a cultural name given to bouts of mania involving infectious erratic dancing, occurrences of which were reported occasionally but passionately from the fourteenth to seventeenth centuries. The phenomenon is sometimes called 'choreomania', from the Greek *choros*, meaning dance, and *mania*, meaning madness. The mania involves being taken over by (usually) temporary madness, sometimes in large groups. Such events seem to have genuinely occurred, with groups of thousands dancing to the point of exhaustion, and the idea took on cultural significance after being depicted by artists including both Breughel the Elder and Younger. Both Breughel depictions show musicians accompanying those in fits of madness and spectators both watching and joining in.

It is tempting to relate the St Vitus dance to Bakhtinian carnival (discussed in Chapter 1), a similarly infectious and unsupressable group eruption into disorder, and yet the St Vitus dance involves real and permanent madness, with participants often becoming very ill. Indeed, the name of St Vitus is given to the dance because he is the patron saint of epilepsy, with which this 'medieval dancing mania' is often associated.[6] The phenomenon continues to divide those who seek to provide social and scientific explanations for medieval madness, but the point is that the severity of the effects on those involved distinguishes it from the joyous atmosphere of Bakhtinian carnival.[7] The St Vitus dance may be considered a much more anxious carnival experience not invested with 'liberating' qualities. Brecht writes here that Hegel's eye twitches as if to recall the 'unsupressable' St Vitus dance, as if there is always a flicker of anxious disorder hidden just behind Hegel's ordered façade, threatening to erupt into chaos at any point. More than this, Brecht stresses the presence of order and disorder not only 'in closest proximity' but 'in one

[5] Bertolt Brecht, *Gessamelte Werke*, vol. 14 (Frankfurt: Suhrkamp, 1967), pp. 1460–61. English translation provided by Mladen Dolar.

[6] See E. R. Dodds, *The Greeks and the Irrational* (London: University of California Press, 1951) and more recently Paul Fung, *Dostoevsky and the Epileptic Mode of Being* (London: Legenda, 2015), pp. 7–9.

[7] See John Waller, 'Looking Back: Dancing Plagues and Mass Hysteria', *The Psychologist*, vol. 22, no. 7 (July 2009), pp. 644–7.

Figure 3.1 Pieter Breughel the Elder, *The Dancing Mania: Pilgrimage of the Epileptics to the Church at Molenbeek*, 1564. Drawing. Held at Albertinium, Vienna.

and the same place', suggesting that the very moment in which totality is asserted is not only threated by disorder but in fact *is* the moment of greatest disorder. Brecht sees this as evidence of the comedian within Hegel and this section explores the idea of laughter as event as a process involving this kind of paradoxical relationship between order and disorder. If laughter is seen as event, it is a moment of both the greatest order and the greatest disorder.

Hegel discusses comedy at some length across his work, though this part of his oeuvre is critically neglected.[8] There is sporadic discussion of comedy in small but important sections of the *Phenomenology*, and in a much more sustained discussion at the end of his last work, the posthumously published *Aesthetics*, Hegel dedicates fifty pages to the topic of comedy. These final fifty pages of his life's work, neglected by criticism, seem to recall stories surrounding Aristotle's lost book on Comedy, the second part of the *Poetics*. Umberto Eco speculates about these lost pages in his 1980 novel *The Name*

[8] Agnes Heller makes an interesting connection between Hegel and the comic novel, though it is by no means the focus of her reading of comedy. See *Immortal Comedy*, p. 93. Alenka Zupančič dedicates a whole chapter to Hegelian comedy in *The Odd One In*, pp. 11–60.

of the Rose, somewhat comically suggesting that discovery of the text that would undo the Western traditions of thought that have been set on their course by Aristotelian philosophy. Hegel, likewise considered by many to be an embodiment of established European rationality, finished his final lecture series with a disruptive and subversive discussion of comedy that has been somewhat 'lost'.

In the late 1820s, towards the end of the series of lectures which ended the year before his death in 1831, Hegel turns to the question of laughter. The definition of comedy he gives here fits neither the idea of comedy as disordering and liberating (Chapter 1) nor ideas of comedy as support for existing ideologies (Chapter 2). Hegel somewhat cryptically writes:

> In comedy there comes before our contemplation, in the laughter in which the characters dissolve everything, including themselves, the victory of their own subjective personality which nevertheless persists self assured.[9]

The definition is complex and appears paradoxical. On the one hand the laugh is completely destructive, since it 'dissolves everything', including the subjects and identities involved, like Baktinian carnival or Bataillian laughter (see Chapter 1). On the other hand, at this same moment we are confronted with the 'victory' of the subject's own 'self-assured' and 'subjective' personality. This element of Hegel's conception of laughter statement contains the Hobbesian 'sudden glory' discussed earlier, a laughter that asserts subject-positions and identities. Yet, the comment is also attentive to the transformative qualities of laughter, that it cannot be straightforwardly seen as the assertion of already existing subject-positions but must be seen as the destruction of old identities and productive of new ones. Still a difficulty remains: laughter can dissolve everything, and yet also assert the subject's self-assured presence.

Hegel later returns to the definition, distinguishing 'the comic as such' from what he sees as a more simple laughter involving merely 'the things people laugh at'. Anticipating the psychoanalytical discussions later on, this distinction seems to involve noticing that while there might be kinds of comedy which simply repeat existing structures by encouraging laughter at the same things again and again, there is another humour which is far more constructive and constitutive. Simon Critchley writes, 'It is important to recognize that not all humour is [liberating], and most of the best jokes are fairly reactionary, or at best, simply serve to reinforce social consensus.'[10] This

9 Hegel, *Aesthetics*, p. 1199.
10 Critchley, *On Humour*, p. 11.

book argues that this distinction is not sustainable and that laughter always does more than simply re-enforce what is already there. However, in this moment it shows Hegel's awareness that laughter can at times be productive of new subjectivities rather than merely reflective of existing ones. This distinction between the 'comic as such' as opposed to the 'things people laugh at' should not be thought of as an elitism in Hegel. He preferred the 'lowbrow' comedy of pantomime, the 'old comedy' of Aristophanes and the 'hodgepodge of merry nonsense' found in 'street ballads' and 'dance' (as he wrote to his wife in 1824) to the 'highbrow' modern comedy of Moliere and others.[11] Perhaps his distinction is anticipating psychoanalytic discussions of comedy with 'an object' and comedy which troubles objectivity, and I pick up this thread in the following chapter.

Of the 'comic as such' Hegel writes that this laughter:

> Implies an infinite light-heartedness and confidence felt by someone raised altogether above his own inner contradiction and not bitter or miserable in it at all: this is the bliss and ease of a man who, being sure of himself, can bear the frustration of his aims and achievements.[12]

This idea of comedy can be read as being on the side of the subject, and on the side of a traditional reading of the Hegelian dialectic and of Hegel's work as asserting totality and completeness. It could be read as asserting that laughter helps the subject overcome its contradiction and progress in some way: there is first the subject, then the subject threated by 'its own inner contradiction', and finally the subject 'raised above' this problem. Yet clearly this reading is insufficient, and the flicker of St Vitus is visible in Hegel's eye, since it has to do not only with the development of a pre-existing contradiction into a total and secure conclusion (thesis, antithesis, synthesis) but with the absolute destruction of what has gone before in the emergence of something new. Hegel returns to the definition of comedy for a third time and stresses the radically destructive function of the laughter. Comedy is:

> When what has no substance in itself has destroyed its show of existence by its own agency, the individual makes himself master of this dissolution too and remains undisturbed in himself and at ease.[13]

[11] G. W. Hegel, *Hegel: The Letters*, trans. Clark Butler and Christiane Seiler (Bloomington: Indiana University Press, 1984), p. 619.

[12] Hegel, *Aesthetics*, p. 1200.

[13] Ibid., p. 1202.

For Hegel, a moment of true comedy destroys something which 'has no substance in itself' and only ever had 'a show of existence'. In its place, something new emerges. This new thing may be thought of as 'truth', as if comedy abolishes appearance and reveals 'true reality' underneath apparent fictions (something laughter studies has often claimed).[14] Something is destroyed and 'dissolved' which is shown never to have had any substance but to have been in the order of appearance only. Yet, the key here is another implication: that the thing that is produced appears to have always been there; rather than appearing new, it seems to 'remain' and to be 'undisturbed', even though it has been produced anew in the moment of comedy. This is a crucial part of the argument here: laughter starts and finishes something, but that which it starts appears to have pre-existed, it 'remains undisturbed' and 'persists self-assured'. These comments about comedy are truly unique and should contribute significantly to existing discussions of comedy. Hegel implies that true comedy is not so much about dismantling appearance and revealing truths but that comedy functions to produce truth itself. Perhaps we can hypothesize that comedy turns existing truths into mere appearance and creates new truths which appear grounded in more than appearance, as indeed truth always appears to be. I will try to bear this out in what follows.

Rather than the *Aesthetics*, where Hegel discussed comedy directly, Brecht singles out *The Science of Logic* as the most comical of Hegel's texts. In that text Hegel explores the idea of a 'beginning', questioning how order comes into being. For Brecht:

> His book 'The Greater Logic' … is one of the great comic works of world literature. It is about the mode of a life of concepts, those slippery, unstable, unaccountable existences; how they insult each other and fight with knives, and then sit down to dinner together as if nothing had happened. They appear, so to speak, in pairs, each is married to its opposite … What order declares is immediately denied, in one and the same breath if possible, by disorder, its inseparable partner.[15]

Brecht's comments on Hegel the comedian can be taken ironically; but together with the comparable comments about Hegel's hidden laughter made by Lacan and Heine, it nevertheless reveals an odd comic potential underside in Hegelian thought.

In *The Science of Logic*, Hegel comments that a whole history of philosophy has been interested in thinking about the beginning only as content; 'earlier

[14] See, for example, Olson, *The Theory of Comedy*, pp. 35–6.

[15] Brecht, *Gessamelte Werke*, vol. 14, pp. 1401–2.

abstract thought is at first only interested in the principle as *content*'.[16] 'Principle' here means that which comes first or that which is primary; content has been privileged as that which comes first. Hegel then comments that subsequent thought has moved towards thinking about the beginning in terms of 'the cognitive process' and subjectivity, the process of mediation or representation, rather than content or materiality. However, for Hegel neither of these ways of thinking of the beginning will suffice. Instead, there is 'a need to unite the method with the content, the form with the principle'. For Hegel, if it is possible to speak of a beginning then we must find there both 'form' and 'content', both 'principle' and 'method'. Hegel qualifies that the word principle is used to refer to the beginning here; 'thus the *principle* ought to be also the beginning'. The word contains both that which was there first, the principle as source, origin or root, and also the principle as 'united with form' to use Hegel's terms, as in the sense of having a principle or law, a form to apply to actions (*OED*). So, he is picking up on a paradox, as with the sentence which follows, which reads: 'that *which has priority* for thinking ought to be also the *first* in the process of thinking'. Here the word priority is of interest to Hegel precisely because of its contradiction; it means both something that comes first, and also something that is in a position of power, which has priority and has therefore been established only in relation to something else which comes after it. Laughter may fit this model: the *cause* of laughter has priority in the sense that it comes first, preceding the event of laughter and its effects. Yet, its status as having priority is only qualified by the event of laughter which follows it.

For Hegel, nothing is as spontaneous as it seems (compare discussions of laughter and spontaneity in Chapter 2). He writes:

> There is nothing in heaven or nature or spirit or anywhere else that does not contain just as much immediacy as mediation, so that both these determinations prove to be unseparated and inseparable and the opposition between them nothing real.[17]

Everything which appears immediate contains just as much mediation, and vice versa, anticipating a Freudian concept of the unconscious. These two things, mediation on the one hand and immediacy on the other, which have characterized all prior theorizations of the beginning, are for Hegel inseparable, although equally importantly, something falsely separates them.

16 Georg Freidrich Hegel, *The Logic of Science*, trans. George di Giovanni (Cambridge: Cambridge University Press, 2010), p. 46.

17 Ibid.

This process which divides the two is close to what we can think of as the beginning or origin in Hegel's work. For Hegel we can say that the beginning does not exist at the beginning, but rather, the beginning is, in Hegel's own words, '*to be* made' by this division.[18] At the beginning there is a divider, something which precedes immediacy and mediation, cause and effect, which separates the two, producing them in relation to each other. The event of laughter can be seen as just such a divider, a rupture that produces both the cause of laughter and its effects, which determines both the object of laughter and the subject laughing. It is this unsecuring sense of how truth and identity come into being which Brecht found so humorous in Hegel and called 'those slippery, unstable, unaccountable existences [that] insult each other and fight with knives, and then sit down to dinner together as if nothing had happened'.

With the more well-known Hegelian concept of the *Aufhebung*, the question of the beginning moves towards what Badiou would later call 'the event'. The *Aufhebung* describes the way in which we move from one thing to another, and as such it is often read as evidence for Hegel's philosophy as a progress narrative that ultimately results in the affirmation of the subject. However, if we approach the *Aufhebung* via Hegel's discussion of the beginning, this reading of Hegel as a philosopher of completion or totality is complicated. The word *Aufhebung* contains the idea of 'annulment' and 'abolishment', suggesting the eradication of what has gone before, and it also means to 'lift-up' or 'sublate', meaning that it has to do with 'synthesis' and moving on, establishing the new in place of the old but preserving the old within it.

In his influential essay 'The Caesura of the Speculative', Phillipe Lacoue-Labarthe offers a rereading of Hegel along these lines, arguing that the idea of a Hegelian synthesis should be seen as a 'caesura' rather than as a development of what has gone before.[19] As with Hegel's concept of the beginning, *Aufhebung* is a break or cut which is formative: it is the break or caesura which destroys what has gone before. It establishes the 'new' in relation to the 'old', but it also establishes the 'old' in relation to the 'new'. This sheds light on how laughter might function: it eradicates the past and establishes a new reality, but the new reality brought into being by laughter has both a (new) past and a (new) present. The best example may be laughing at our own former mistakes. The process of laughing at ourselves creates a former self who is laughed at and

[18] Ibid.

[19] Phillipe Lacoue-Labarthe, 'The Caesura of the Speculative', in *Typography: Mimesis, Philosophy, Politics*, ed. Christopher Fynsk (Massachusetts: Harvard University Press, 1989), pp. 208–35.

a new self who is capable of laughing in this way, neither of whom existed in this form before the laughter. Recently *Huffington Post* published an article in praise of those able to laugh at themselves and it inadvertently pointed to how many political figures build their identities in this way, listing Bill Clinton, Hilary Clinton and Barrack Obama. We can add George W. Bush and Boris Johnson to a list that could easily go on: politicians seem to use this 'caesural' quality in laughter to modify their public identities, eradicating their former identities and producing new ones defined by the capacity to laugh at the old.

This connects laughter with the more dominant notion of 'negation' in Hegel's thought. Connecting Hegelian negation with Freud and Lacan, psychoanalyst Wilfried Ver Eecke explores how negation 'plays a crucial function in an individual's attempt to reach the truth about himself or herself'.[20] Using Hegel's idea of the emergence of self-consciousness, Eecke explores how Hegel's conception of the process leads to a desired and constructive outcome, whereas Freudian 'denial' leads to an undesired and regressive outcome. In Hegelian negation the subject emerges (as in his comments on comedy) unscathed and somehow developed. The abovementioned examples show laughter-as-negation functioning constructively in this Hegelian way, but such negation is also dialectical, working to unsecure the subject it brings into being by showing it to be in constant unfixed process (comparable to how caricature may erase the original, discussed earlier). David Gray Carlson explains, 'The very idea of negation refers to a past. If I say that Being is not, I am also saying Being once was, because negation always works on some positive entity that preceded it.'[21] Dialectical reasoning involves a 'remembering', 'a kind of fantasy time' which is not chronology but which recalls a past. Carlson puts it well in saying that this dialectical reasoning 'embarrasses the Understanding by recalling the history of the concept. It remembers that the supposedly immediate concept was mediated after all.'[22] Such is the dialectical and threatening underside of a subject asserted anew in a moment of comedy. Just as the subject moves forward, dialectical reasoning 'embarrasses the Understanding by pointing out that the opposite is just as true: Being turns into Nothing. It has "ceased to be."' This may leave the anxious residue found even in the most self-assertive comedy, an idea picked up in Chapter 4.

20 Wilfried Ver Eecke, *Denial, Negation, and the Forces of the Negative* (Albany: SUNY Press, 2016), p. 39.

21 David Gray Carlson, *A Commentary to Hegel's Science of Logic* (London: Palgrave, 2007), p. 17.

22 Ibid., p. 21.

The caesura is the domain of Hegel's contemporary and personal friend Freidrich Hölderlin (1770–1843), with whom Hegel shared a room while studying in Tubingen in 1790. Hölderlin theorizes the concept of the caesura in the following way:

> In the rhythmic sequence of the representations wherein transport presents itself, there becomes necessary what in poetic meter is called *caesura*, the pure word, the counter-rhythmic rupture; namely, in order to meet the onrushing change of representations at its highest point in such a manner that very soon there does not appear the change of representation but the representation itself.[23]

The caesura is a break, interruption or interval, but not a break in an otherwise continuous trajectory. Lacoue-Labarthe describes the *Aufhebung* as caesura for exactly this reason; the *Aufhebung*, like the caesura, is the imposition of a new way of thinking, but rather than a synthesis, the caesura destroys what has gone before, breaking from it and establishing something new. It is an event which 'comes to meet the onrushing charge of representations', says Hölderlin, so that what happens before the caesura is already rushing towards it, anticipating it and governed by the caesura as its *future*. It is not that the caesura interrupts an otherwise stable or linear series of representations but that those representations themselves are conditioned by the caesura which is coming to meet them.

Of this passage in Hölderlin, Walter Benjamin remarked, 'Its fundamental significance for the theory of art in general, beyond serving as the basis for a theory of tragedy, seems not yet to have been recognized.'[24] Jeremy Tambling glosses the concept of caesura in Hölderlin and its development in Benjamin:

> The caesura may be traumatic, a radical undoing of subjectivity, perhaps even the condition of modern madness. But since the shock and caesural and traumatic may not be the same, the caesural may lead into the other scene, the power of the other, what constitutes the text, the *Gedichtete*. It turns back to ask what language it is which is at the origin.[25]

[23] Friedrich Hölderlin, 'Remarks on Oedipus', in *Essays and Letters on Theory*, ed. and trans. Thomas Pfau (Albany: SUNY Press, 1988), pp. 101–8 (pp. 101–2).

[24] Walter Benjamin, *Selected Writings, Volume One: 1913–1926*, ed. Marcus Bullock and Michael W. Jennings (Cambridge, MA: Harvard University Press, 2014), p. 340.

[25] Jeremy Tambling, *Hölderlin and the Poetry of Tragedy: Readings of Sophocles, Shakespeare, Nietzsche and Benjamin* (Eastbourne: Sussex University Press, 2014), p. 26.

This idea of the caesura again helps to see the peculiar work that laughter does; laughter can be seen as a caesura, both formative and destructive, ending something and producing something, rushing towards the subject and transforming both its past and future. That which it ends and that which it begins can only be thought of in relation to each other, and can only be thought of at all because of the caesura that separates them. Past and present are created by a dividing caesura that establishes the relation between them. In his remarks on Antigone, Hölderlin describes the difference between Antigone and Oedipus using two small diagrams:

> The rule, the calculable law of 'Antigone' compares to that of 'Oedipus' like ——/—— to ——\—— so that the balance inclines more from the beginning toward the end than from the end toward the beginning.[26]

Hölderlin explains that the slash represents the caesura, which he also calls 'the counterrhythmic rupture'. It is a kind of event which interrupts, and which controls not only what follows it but what comes before as well. Hölderlin says that in the case of *Antigone*, it makes it seem as though 'the first half were protected from the second' whereas in *Oedipus*, it appears as if the first half is attacking the second half that needs protecting. The point is that the interruption is needed to constitute either side. In the trajectory of our identities laughter operates like this little line in Hölderlin, splicing our subjectivity apart and reconstituting it by creating its past and present.

This idea of *Aufhebung* as caesura then, explains its simultaneously destructive and constructive functions. In a similar way, Derrida connects the *Aufhebung* to psychoanalysis, seeing the notion of the *Aufhebung* in Hegel as a concept which anticipates what Freud would later call repression.[27] The process of *Aufhebung* is one of order and rational control, since it establishes one way of thinking over others, but Derrida argues that it is also fundamentally anti-rational. Suzanne Gearhart puts it nicely when she says that for Derrida 'the process of *Aufhebung* also escapes rationality or lies beyond it, in the sense that the reason that it constitutes cannot be there from the beginning to control that process'.[28] For Derrida this can be brought to bear on psychoanalysis, pointing to a radical capacity of psychoanalytic thought that Derrida is often elsewhere critical of; 'repression can be thought

26 Hölderlin, 'Remarks on Oedipus', pp. 101–2.

27 Jacques Derrida, *Glas*, trans. R. Rand (Nebraska: University of Nebraska Press, 1986), pp. 190–91.

28 Suzanne Gearhart, 'The Remnants of Philosophy: Psychoanalysis after *Glas*', in *Hegel after Derrida*, ed. Stuart Barnett (London: Routledge, 1998), pp. 147–70 (p. 156).

of as the dialectic'.[29] The dialectic must be thought of as repression because in the process of the *Aufhebung* reason emerges not through consciousness but through what is not known, what is unconscious. The point here is that the dialectic, and repression, cannot be 'thought', so that what changes in the *Aufhebung* is not conscious thought but the constitution of the unconscious, or the constitution of both in relation to each other, so that rationality emerges from repression and therefore cannot have been there to govern the process in the first place: rationality arises out of nothing, or with nothing to guarantee it. Despite this, it *appears* to be evidence of its own existence, and inevitable.

Jean-Luc Nancy suggests, in a short essay, that laughter may be the phenomenon most radically affected by this realization. Speaking of Hegel and of Derrida on Hegel, Nancy puts it nicely when, of laughter, he writes that 'what makes sense about meaning is that it senses itself making sense'.[30] If we can say that laughter is a 'beginning' or 'caesura' that produces something which it appears to reflect, then what is specific about laughter is that it senses its role in the production of a cause which seems to have pre-existed, rather than believing in itself as an effect of already existing objects, identities and subject-positions. Laughter, with all its anxieties, knows that what it brings into being is completely unsecured and always potentially subject to complete change.

Louis Althusser, anticipating his friend Lacan but who 'never went to one of Lacan's seminars' because the room was 'full of people and thick with smoke', sees Hegel's work as that of the 'event', albeit a pre-Badiouian one.[31] On the first page of his book on Hegel, as the first thing he wants to say about Hegel, Althusser writes:

> Hegel's philosophy presents itself not only as a corpus of truths, a finished whole ... but also as a totalizing whole; not only an attempt to grasp reality, but also as the act by which truth is fulfilled or accomplished ... Not merely the revelation of this event, but the event itself.[32]

It is this observation which shows how comic Hegel's work is and how close it is to laughter, to the destructive laughter of the St Vitus dance, which goes

[29] Derrida, *Glas*, p. 191.

[30] Nancy, 'Elliptical Sense', p. 177. See also Jean-LucNancy, 'Wild Laughter in the Throat of Death', *MLN*, vol. 103, no. 4 (September 1987), pp. 719–36.

[31] See his autobiography, *The Future Lasts a Long Time*, ed. Olivier Corpet and Yann Moulier Boutang, trans. Richard Veasey (London: Vintage, 1994), p. 186; Louis Althusser, *The Spectre of Hegel: Early Writings*, ed. Francois Matheron, trans. G. M. Goshgarian (London: Verso, 2014), p. 23.

[32] Althusser, *The Spectre of Hegel*, p. 23.

far beyond the liberating qualities of carnival and confronts rationality itself on the precipice, to Brecht's sense that order and disorder appear in the same moment and yet we sit down to dinner again as if nothing has happened. As the philosopher of 'truths' and of the 'finished whole', Hegel is the figure of rationality and of the attempt to rationally 'grasp reality'. Yet his work does not discover rationality and reality that are already there. Rather, his work is 'also the act by which truth is fulfilled or accomplished', the 'event itself' which causes rationality and order to emerge. As such it functions like Derrida's idea of *Aufhebung* as repression or Nancy's claim that the *Aufhebung* 'senses itself making sense', coming into being in the very moment it asserts its unruffled and secure totality and therefore indicating its own insecurity. Describing Hegel as the most anxious of men, his student Heinrich Heine makes the following comment which chimes with that of Brecht many years later:

> I often saw how he anxiously looked around, fearing that people would understand him. He liked me a lot since he was certain I wouldn't betray him; I even thought at the time that he was servile. When I was once uneasy about the saying 'all that is, is rational', he smiled in a peculiar way and remarked: 'This could also read 'all that is rational must be'. He quickly looked around, but soon calmed down.[33]

As Mladen Dolar has written, the passage shows Hegel as 'someone who must constantly attempt to hide his subversive underside'.[34] This subversive underside is to do with laughter. Hegel's manner is uneasy and anxious because he fears being understood, seemingly on this particular point. To Heine he comments that "all that is, is rational' could also read 'all that is rational must be'. While the first phrase implies that being is rational, the second indicates that this is because rationality demands to *be*. He sees in the very act of making rationality inevitable, the strange and powerful way in which rationality demands to be inevitable and makes itself so, undoing the very thing he stands for. This is the true St Vitus in the eye of Hegel and it makes its presence felt in a 'peculiar smile' that threatens laughter.

While it was Georges Bataille who wrote 'my philosophy is a philosophy of laughter' (see intro) and Hegel would never have described his own work in this way, it is the philosopher of rationality whose work simultaneously

33 Heinrich Heine, 'Briefe über Deutschland', in *Sämtliche Schriften*, vol. 5 (Munich: Hanser, 1976), p. 197. I have used the translation of this passage given by Mladen Dolar in 'The Owl of Minerva from Dusk till Dawn, or, Two Shades of Gray', *Filozofija i društvo*, vol. 26, no. 4 (2015), pp. 875–90 (pp. 882–3).

34 Dolar, 'The Owl of Minerva', p. 883.

undoes it.[35] While Bataille saw laughter as 'non-knowledge' or anti-knowledge, Hegel's philosophy, and his laughter, was both at once, 'in one and the same place!' Hegel's philosophy was fundamentally comic because it unsecured what it brought into being at the same moment, establishing a reality but showing that reality to be established in that moment. In this sense, Badiou's later concept of the event, an interruption of traditional ideas of dialectical time in Hegel, might have its basis in Hegelian thought itself. Regarding the subject of this book, I will take forward from this discussion the following question: is it not possible that *all* laughter works in this Hegelian way, appearing to be a response to what already exists but in fact establishing a new reality while simultaneously making the claim that this reality has always been there merely waiting to be grasped or seen?

Laughter and psychoanalytic time: Freud and Lacan

While for Brecht it was Hegel's *Logic* which held within it the greatest humour, for Lacan it was the *Phenomenology* that he found 'hysterically funny'. Frustrated with his student's failure to pick upon his suggestions, Lacan says:

> It has no kind of effect ... if I say to you that *The Phenomonology of Spirit* is hysterically funny. And yet, this is what it is. (*S17*: 170)

Frustrated by a lack of attention to the importance of Hegel's humour, Lacan hides his insight in a throwaway comment here, himself making a joke since he has deliberately made it easy for his audience to ignore him in the very statement he accuses them of doing so. 'Hysterically funny' means not just very funny but that Hegel's comedy must be thought of in terms of the 'discourse of the hysteric', something he suggested weeks earlier in the seminar (*S17*: 23). For Lacan, Hegel's discourse goes against the history of philosophy, which has been nothing but 'a fascinating enterprise for the master's benefit'. On the contrary, with Hegel's 'outrageous absolute knowledge', we confront the fact that 'what leads to knowledge ... is the hysteric's discourse' (*S17*: 23). The hysteric's discourse is a constantly questioning, never fixed sense of knowledge. The idea of knowledge on the precipice is recalled and the St Vitus dance is indeed 'hysterical' both in terms of humour and in terms of

[35] Georges Bataille, 'Nonknowledge, Laughter, and Tears', in *The Unfinished System of Nonknowledge*, ed. Stuart Kendall, trans. Michelle Kendall and Stuart Kendall (Minneapolis: University of Minnesota, 2001), p. 138.

the hysteric's discourse. For Lacan, Hegel counters the idea that knowledge is fixed and confronts the fact that knowledge is always new. Truths are produced rather than reflecting what is already there, as discussed earlier. This, for Lacan, is 'hysterically funny', with the pun fully intended.

Freud did not consider himself much indebted to Hegel and it is Lacan who brings Hegel formally into psychoanalytic discourse. A Lacanian Hegel is something that has been emphasized by Slavoj Žižek, Mladen Dolar and Alenka Zupančič, but it is important that this against the grain reading of Hegel was a part of Lacan's work already. Lacan criticizes traditional philosophy and makes Hegel the absolute antithesis of this (*S17*: 23). Influenced by Kojeve's lectures on Hegel that he attended in the 1930s, Lacan criticizes ideas of the ego-as-origin which characterize the psychoanalysis of Anna Freud and other Freudian schools. Distancing himself from these schools, Lacan writes that 'one should not imagine that [psychoanalysis] is something that would be the discovery of being or of the soul'.[36] Lacan, like Hegel, asks not what the origin of the subject is but rather how we are formed as subjects who see ourselves as originary.[37] Ian Parker and David Pavon-Cuellar explain that 'Lacanian discourse analysis' is an attempt to move away from models which 'attempt to go back to some reality that was expressed, represented or reflected in discourse' and instead place the emphasis is on 'the reality of discourse itself', not just linguistics but the way in which real subjects are produced and constructed within those languages.[38] Lacan's comment about Hegel's humour is no throwaway remark but a central point of Seminar 17 to which he repeatedly returns.

> All the way through – take as an example what Hegel is able to say about culture – the most pertinent remarks concerning the play of events and exercises of wit abound. I repeat, there is nothing more amusing. (*S17*: 171)

Lacan stresses that *reason*, the very thing affirmed by Hegel, operates in his work as a cunning trick; 'the cunning of reason is, he tells us, what directed the entire game'. 'However,' writes Lacan, 'the high point of this cunning is not where one thinks it is. It is the cunning of reason, no doubt, but one has to recognize the cunning of the reasoned and take one's hat off to him.'

[36] Jacques Lacan, 'The Tokyo Discourse', *Journal for Lacanian Studies*, vol. 3, no. 1 (2005), pp. 129–44 (p. 3).

[37] Alexandre Kojeve, *Introduction to the Reading of Hegel*, ed. Allan Bloom, trans. James H. Nichols, Jr (New York: Basic Books, 1969).

[38] David Pavon-Cuellar and Ian Parker, *Lacan, Discourse, Event: New Psychoanalytic Approaches to Textual Indeterminacy* (London: Routledge, 2013), p. 2.

Lacan then refers to the 'extraordinarily dirty trick of *The Phenomenology of Spirit*', arguing that Hegel's question 'which is truth?' and 'what brings him into play?' are humorous ones.

Such a point can be situated in relation to the Hegelian line of influence in Lacan's work. Wilfried Ver Eecke has shown how Lacan's fundamental idea of the mirror stage (more in Chapter 4) has its roots in a Hegelian concept of self. Eecke explains:

> Hegel's analysis of the master-and-slave dialectic does not require the hypothesis of two human races [as it did for Schelling], for it presents the inequality between men as emerging from within man himself. The will to overcome this inequality then provides, for Hegel, the driving force for the making of history. The history-creating possibility of this passage in Hegel's *Phenomenology* did not escape Kojeve, the forceful commentator who introduced Hegel to a generation of French intellectuals, including Lacan.[39]

Thus, from Kojeve Lacan took this Hegelian idea of a dialectal creation of man whereby his emergence as subject is based on his emergence as inadequate subject.[40] In other words, there is a dirty trick at the origin of subjectivity whereby the birth of the subject is also the birth of the subject's failure. This could account for the degree of humour that Lacan finds at the heart of Hegelian thought. The birth of the subject and the birth of truth is a humorous topic for Lacan because it shows something coming into existence which conceives of itself as solid and unchangeable but which in the very act of 'coming into existence' is shown to be quite the opposite: produced, contingent and temporary.

Lacan's use of jokes in his seminars, lightly present in these remarks but more striking elsewhere, are important for seeing how his philosophy and his humour function together. Lacan's humour has rarely if even been mentioned (except perhaps by those like Noam Chomsky, who saw Lacan as an arrogant charlatan). Like most jokes, they are usually seen as a 'light' aside to the serious development of his arguments. On the contrary, his use of jokes supplies illustration of how Lacan's thinking works. There may well be an arrogance to them in fact, since he uses them to prove himself right, but in

39 Wilfried Ver Eecke, 'Hegel as Lacan's Source for Necessity in Psychoanalytic Theory', in *Interpreting Lacan*, ed. Joseph H. Smith and William Kerrigan (London: Yale, 1983), pp. 113–38 (p. 118).

40 'Dialectic' was the term used by Kojece in this context. See Kojeve, *Introduction to the Reading of Hegel*, p. 9.

doing so he shows how ideologically powerful jokes can be; how the making of a joke can establish an argument as a truth. Lacan writes, for example:

> Marie-Claire Boons would even give us to understand that ... in some way psychoanalysis frees us from the law.
>
> Fat chance. I am well aware that this is the register in which a libertarian hook attaches itself to psychoanalysis ... The father's death ... does not seem to me to be of a kind to liberate us from it, far from it. (*S17*: 119)

Lacan stresses that psychoanalysis, from Freud's own work to his own, should not be thought of as on the side of liberation (*S17*: 119). Rather, its interest is in the *always structured* movement from one 'discourse' to another, with the production of new subjects and discourses out of and in place of old ones. The joke, turning on the phrase 'fat chance', takes as its target the idea that 'psychoanalysis frees us from the law'. As such, by mocking the idea of liberation, it also targets the idea that humour operates as a 'liberating release', which as discussed in Chapter 1, is often considered to characterize Freud's own theory of humour in *Jokes and their Relation to the Unconscious*. Lacan uses the joke to make a certain event-like movement happen in the very text of his seminar. The laughter (albeit brief) that we might assume accompanied this phrase 'fat chance' in the lecture theatre full of Lacan fanatics is itself a evental change; it turns a reading of psychoanalysis (that of Marie-Claire Boons, who thought that psychoanalysis may liberate us from the law) into a *past* that is now laughed *at* and shown to have only ever had 'a show of existence', to borrow Hegel's language from the previous section. In relation to this past a new present is established in which it is made clear that psychoanalysis is 'far from' liberating. The process therefore establishes a *new* present in relation to this *equally new* past, both of which emerge as the joke is made.

Another way of putting this might be to say that Lacanian psychoanalysis (like laughter) is not about truths but about myths; it does not reveal the 'truth' but shows us the truth of discourse itself. Lacan makes more jokes to hammer home this point:

> Bullshitting, as I have always said, is truth. They are identical ... Why is this privilege given to myth in psychoanalysis? ... Claude Levi-Strauss states the complete myth of Oedipus [but] one can see that it concerns something quite different from whether or not one is going to fuck one's mummy. (*S17*: 111)

This is far more than the point often made by Lacanians that the Oedipus myth is not to be taken literally but metaphorically. Rather than being a myth which shows us something true, it is the mythic status of Oedipus which makes it important. Here, the joke about fucking one's mummy actually does what Lacan describes. The joke shows that we are wrong to see psychoanalysis as something which reaches back into childhood to find 'truths', indicating instead that it is the myths we tell ourselves (about childhood, for example) which are important. These myths, in being shown for the myths that they are (or shown to be 'bullshit') are revealed to have never had anything but a 'show of existence', to borrow Hegel's phrase once more, and a new truth is erected in its place, which then seems to have always been the truth waiting to be revealed by the abolishment of myth.

Which 'truth' is abolished to thc status of myth here? It is the myth that fucking our mothers is at the root of psychoanalysis, a former psychoanalytic 'truth'. Yet the joke does not reveal essential truth (what psychoanalysis is *really* about), but it produces new truth in place of the old myth. This new equally mythic truth appears true by virtue of its comparison with the old abolished myth. Thus Lacan is able to defend Freud, to get him off the hook, and re-establish his theory as a new truth: from this joke on, psychoanalysis was *never* just about 'fucking one's mummy', and Freud *always* meant something quite different. Marie Claire Boons becomes the new mythical past of psychoanalysis, with Lacanian thought its new 'truth', which is revealed by the event that is this joke. It is the same 'dirty trick' played by Hegel's *Phenomenology* and which Lacan found so humorous. Now playing this dirty trick on his seminar audience, Lacan shows that laughter functions to turn established truths into appearance and establish new truths its place.

There is something important about this particular 'humorous' use of a philosopher or thinker from the past. In one of the important books written on Lacan, Jean-Claude Milner writes:

> It is not, therefore, appropriate to present Lacan in a way that would bind it within its own internal logic – consistent or not – and that exposes it completely so that any misinterpretations are corrected. My intention is another entirely: not to clarify Lacan's thoughts, nor to rectify what has been said about it, but to express clearly that there is thought in Lacan's work. Thought, by which I mean something whose existence imposes on those who haven't thought it.[41] (my translation)

[41] Jean-Claude Milner, *L'Œuvre claire: Lacan, la science, la philosophie* (Paris: Éditions du Seuil, 1995), p. 8.

Milner wants to return to Lacan much as Lacan himself returned to Freud, not to develop a totalizing and complete theory but to show how his work reveals problems with or gaps in what has been said up to this point. Lacan said of Freud that he was read 'as one can read anything new … pulling it completely to the side of already accepted notions'.[42] Instead, he wanted to revisit Freud in order to see what his work does which cannot be reconciled with existing thought. Milner could have made the same points about Lacan's use of Hegel. Lacan writes that we ought to 'perceive where the Hegelian construction gapes, remains gaping, and has been closed up in a forced way' (*S17*: 51). It is equally true that Hegel in turn did this to Heraclitus, reading him 'against the grain', and making a claim about his work that countered traditional interpretations, abolishing them as myth and setting up his own interpretation in the guise of truth. What we see here is a 'retroactive' relationship between philosophers which depends on their humour. The revelation of 'truth' in the former philosopher plays a 'dirty trick' on the reader by establishing this truth as already present in the former philosopher, making it seem as though the newly emerged truth has always been their waiting to be 'discovered'.

This peculiar type of 'discovery' is a central concept in Lacanian psychoanalysis. Speaking of moments such as parapraxis, dreams and jokes, Lacan describes an 'impediment, failure, split' which makes its presence felt. 'In a spoken or written sentence something stumbles,' writes Lacan, 'what occurs, what is *produced* in this gap, is presented as *the discovery*' (*S11*: 25). This moment produces something new but appears to discover something old. The Lacanian discovery, as Jeremy Tambling explains, is linked to the work of Surrealist writer Andre Breton, whom Freud met in 1921.[43] The idea originates in Freud's concept of *Nachträglichkeit*, sometimes translated as 'afterwardsness'. *Nachträglichkeit* is deferred action, or perhaps better, retroactive action. Rather than a later reaction to an earlier event, as it is sometimes considered to be, it is a recognition that when the second event occurs the first event is invested with a new significance which turns it into that which it will then always already have been. As a result of its indebtedness to *nachträglichkeit* Lacan says that 'the discovery is *of a strange temporality*'. In its movement, something is produced as a kind of effect which appears to have already been there to function as a cause of what was to come, shattering the expected relationship between cause and effect. What is 'presented' as a finding, is in fact 'produced', what appears to *cause* the discovery by making

[42] Lacan, 'The Tokyo Discourse', p. 32.

[43] Jeremy Tambling, *Literature and Psychoanalysis* (Manchester: Manchester University Press, 2012), pp. 111–12.

revealing itself is in fact an *effect* of it. Laughter can be thought of as exactly this experience. Even Thomas Hobbes's most famous definition of laughter contains an unconscious recognition of this retroactive function of laughter. Hobbes's famous line runs:

> Laughter is nothing else but a sudden glory arising from some sudden conception of some eminency in ourselves, by comparison with the infirmities of others, or with our own formerly.[44]

The 'sudden conception of some eminency in ourselves' is a version of the 'discovery', and laughter appears to be the result of suddenly discovering some eminency in ourselves. It is not difficult to see that the process of laughter is also responsible for producing this superiority *anew*, establishing the identity of the 'laugher' in relation to the object of laughter (more on this in Chapter 4). Hobbes is frequently cited as the proponent of laughter as superiority, of the idea that laughter affirms one person over another, but the last part of Hobbes's famous definition is always entirely ignored in these discussions. The additional comment 'or with our own formerly' is where the interesting point of Hobbes's argument is found. It not only shows that there are more complex elements to Hobbesian laughter than the affirmation of one person over another but that Hobbes noticed the 'strange temporality' of laughter. His comment knows that laughter changes us and therefore allows us to be compared with our former selves, but that this newly produced subjectivity appears to already to be there to be suddenly conceived of.

Laughter and 'the event': Alain Badiou

The connection between laughter and the event is one that has been made in various anticipatory ways throughout this book. The event, a concept which finds its culmination in the work of Alain Badiou, is closely related to the Hegelian conception of a beginning and of *Aufhebung*, and it brings these ideas together with psychoanalytic discussions of time and retroactivity, combining psychoanalysis with Hegelianism. Part of the conceptual framework of the book has been to show that Badiou's 'interruption' of dialectical time in Hegel was anticipated by Hegel as well. As an extension, it has also been to show that laughter has been present through the history of the concept of the event, from its origin in Hegel to its culmination in

[44] Hobbes, *Leviathan*, p. 34.

Badiou. The event is the moment at which something happens, at which, as I discussed earlier in relation to the caesura, history becomes readable, or is constituted; a moment at which representation appears. It a moment which produces something that seems to have always been there waiting to be found, negotiating and redefining the past and present in relation to each other. Of course, laughter is not the only discourse that functions like this and it may be that all representation can operate in this evental way, modifying and constructing that which it presents while appearing to discover or represent it. In what follows I hope to consolidate the argument that laughter bears a special and specific relationship to the idea of the event. Laughter involves a repetition of this evental process found in many kinds of discourse, which draws attention to the process happening, potentially undoing it or at least showing that the course of history is malleable and subject to transformation. As I have said earlier, I am using the terms 'evental' and 'eventally' in this technical sense which I have outlined. In what follows and in what remains of the book, I use these terms with the specific Badiouian implications of the words, discussed here in detail.

The concept of the event would not have developed without the influence of Freud's idea of *nachträglichkeit*, and Ian Parker and David Pavon-Cuellar make a connection between *Nachträglichkeit* and the 'event' in their book *Lacan, Discourse, Event*. Parker and Pavon-Cuellar explain:

> The event is something that takes form for us within the symbolic 'after the event' according to the logic of 'deferred action', '*apres coup*', what Freud originally spoke about as 'Nachträglich'. This is a peculiarly psychoanalytic conception of time, a looping back and activation of what has already occurred, and the investment of that first event with a significance that turns it into what it will later always already be.[45]

Andrew Benjamin's book on the event makes a similar point, that *nachträglichkeit* is involved when what we are dealing with 'cannot be adequately formulated in chronological terms'.[46] Because the event modifies the past retroactively, its function cannot be described in linear language. Furthermore, seeing the event as *nachträglichkeit* means that the term event designates not only major world events or historical revolutions but

[45] Ian Parker and David Pavon-Cuellar, 'Lacanian Domains of Practice and Forms of Event in Analysis', in *Lacan, Discourse, Event*, ed. Ian Parker and David Pavon-Cuéllar (London: Routledge, 2013), pp. 338–46 (p. 338).

[46] Andrew Benjamin, *The Plural Event: Descartes, Hegel, Heidegger* (London: Routledge, 2005), p. 21.

the relationship between occurrences and their representations in a much broader sense. Lacan noted the prevalence of this evental mechanism in all representation, commenting that 'language has, if you care to put it like that, a sort of retrospective effect in determining what is ultimately decided to be real'.[47] It is possible and somewhat useful to read the event in terms of major historical occurrences; the events of the Holocaust, for example, have retroactively changed the entire history of reading Fascism, bringing its qualities into being and turning previous manifestations of Fascism into the structures that led to its ultimate realization. Lacan's point, though, is that all language operates in this evental way; that every utterance has the potential to change any previous ones into what they then seem to have always already been.

Deriving much from Hegel and the *Aufhebung*, Badiou's concept of the event takes it out of the idea of a causal and chronological chain. For Badiou, one cannot think only about the causes of the event, or the factors which make up the event; the event is not just an effect of a cause, not just something that takes its place on a linear timeline where A precedes B. Instead, 'a site is only evental insofar as it is retroactively qualified as such by the occurrence of an event' and 'there is no event save relative to an historical situation'.[48] In a sense, it is Badiou's claim that all events exist only in relation to other events. This means that a second event is needed to turn the first event into an event. In traditional philosophies of causality (e.g. progress narratives and traditional readings of Hegel), any event A seems to contain within it, as a future, the possibility of event B. This means that whatever event occurs must contain within it all the possible 'future' events which may or may not occur subsequently. On its most basic level something like the big bang theory would fit this structure; it is a theory that considers event A to hold within it the possibilities of all future events. On the contrary, for Badiou, as for Hegel, event A only becomes an event in relation to event B, which it is constituted in relation to. The moment of 'the event', then, requires a caesura, the break which divides the two events, creating the relationship between them and constituting both. If event A leads to event B, then both A and B are changed by this relation, so that event B equally leads to event A.

Between events A and B, and between cause and effect, is an invisible and inarticulable void or divider, a differentiator which separates form from content, cause from effect, subject from representation, and in doing so it is ceasurally productive of both sides of this divide. Badiou reminds us of

47 Lacan, 'Some Reflections on the Ego', p. 3.

48 Alain Badiou, *Being and Event*, trans. Oliver Feltham (London: Continuum, 2005), p. 179.

this point that 'it is essential to remember that no term within a situation designates the void'.[49] For Badiou the event is neither 'the one', the thing which is symbolized, nor 'the multiple', everything which it is not. Rather it is the gap between the two which constitutes both in relation to each other. Žižek writes, 'The *space* of an event is that which opens up the gap that separates an effect from its causes.'[50] Laughter operates in this way, between cause and effect, separating and constituting both. When we laugh our laughter is never divorced from its cause because it is a kind of divider between cause and (often largely unknown) effects. Laughter always has causes, but it also always has the capacity to exceed its causes, modifying chronologies and structures around the subject.

A whole history of discussion has defended and celebrated laughter as positive, but if it is to be connected to the event then it cannot be seen in this way: an event is neither good nor bad. Instead, its effects can be completely various depending on the conditions of its event. As Badiou stresses, the event is always biased; as I have argued earlier about laughter, laughter is never neutral or free of ideological agendas. Badiou writes; 'there are no natural events, nor are their neutral events'.[51] Likewise, there is no natural laughter, nor is there neutral laughter. Events always condition the past and the present, and they are deeply ideological. Laughter as event is an argument that laughter is similarly ideological.

With laughter, as in an event, ideology is being produced, and an entire past and present is being restructured and recreated. Yet, in making this process apparent to us, the whole system becomes unsecured, provisional. It has the potential to show that the reality we are brought within by the event is mythical and produced rather than essential and fixed. As discussed earlier, Jean-Luc Nancy describes the same process in Hegel and Derrida as 'sense sensing itself coming into being'. Elsewhere Nancy describes laughter, which can now be thought of in these terms:

> The origin is laughing … It laughs at the peal of its laughter, we might say. Which is not to say that it is unserious or that it is painless. It is beyond all opposition of serious and nonserious, of pain and pleasure. Or rather, it is at the juncture of these oppositions, at the limit which they share and which itself is only the limit of each of these terms, the limit of their signification, the limit to which these significations, as

[49] Ibid., p. 56.
[50] Žižek, *Event*, p. 4.
[51] Badiou, *Being and Event*, p. 178.

> such, are exposed. One could say that such a limit … is the place of the sublime. I prefer to say … that it is the place of exposition.[52]

Laughter is an origin, it is prior to its cause and its effect, and it is 'the juncture of these oppositions': it creates them. And here we can see the double function of laughter which this chapter has been driving at throughout. It is both ideological, and the moment where ideology can be undone, or shown for what it is, at which its lack of control can be revealed. Badiou's work is concerned with the way the event produces truths. Laughter is exactly such an event. As Peter Hallward writes, Badiou's work is interested in 'the process by which a … truth may eventually produce verifiable components of a new knowledge, a new way of understanding the parts of a situation'.[53] With laughter we are right at the heart of ideology; laughter is an instance of ideology coming into being; it creates a cause and effect, and it establishes them as already having been there. And yet with laughter we are shown this happening, we sense it coming into being, or at least we can do. In this way laughter is the event, the place of exposition, meaning the opening out or abandonment to chance (*OED*). It is productive, and what it produces may control us and dictate our thoughts, but it can recognize itself as this moment of juncture which forms thought, showing that no ideology is in charge, that nothing is there to control it.

Žižek asks; 'is an event a change in the way reality appears to us, or is it a shattering transformation of reality itself?'[54] The point I hope to have arrived at through Lacan and Badiou is that the two can be one and the same; in changing the way that reality appears to us, reality is retroactively changed. Laughter as an event transforms the way we see reality and transforms reality itself. Discussing Saint Paul, Badiou emphasizes that 'the Christian subject does not pre-exist the event he declares (the resurrection); what he was before is of no importance.[55] Likewise, it is argued here that laughter is an event in that it bears this relationship to subjectivity; every laugh transforms and produces the subject in new ways changing both its perception and its reality. What the subject was before the laugh is also created by the laugh so that there is no outside to the world that is forged by laughter. In this way laughter has much in common with other such 'events'. Yet unlike other events, laughter senses the sense it produces coming into being, giving it the potential to unsecure the very anchor of ideology at

[52] Nancy, 'Elliptical Sense', p. 180.
[53] Peter Hallward, *Badiou: A Subject to Truth* (London: University of Minnesota Press, 2003), p. 109.
[54] Žižek, *Event*, p. 5.
[55] Hallward, *Badiou*, p. 110.

the same moment. In other words, *laughter is an event that can show itself as an event.*

'I can laugh': Kafka's letters

The following discussion develops these discussions in various ways via a sustained example, a single experience of laughter detailed in a letter of Franz Kafka.[56] The quotations that follow are in the chronological order in which they appear in Kafka's letter, but I break regularly throughout the letter to discuss the elements of humour in each section.[57] The letter begins:

> I can also laugh, Felice, have no doubt about this: I am even known as a great laugher, although in this respect I used to be far crazier than I am now.[58]

The first sentence of Kafka's letter implicates the reader in a complex consideration of the effects of laughter. The connection between laughter and identity in the first 'I can also laugh, Felice' is itself suggestive, as is the idea of being known as a 'great laugher'. The claim 'I can laugh' draws attention to the Hegelian 'beginning' found in laughter: Kafka's joke points to the fact that that a laugh itself (in place of this comment 'I can laugh') would operate both as a replacement for the claim 'I can laugh' and as proof of its validity. A laugh transforms the subject into a 'laugher' (while a great laugh or a great many laughs turn the subject into a 'great laugher'), and it appears to show a potentiality or propensity for laughter in the subject which has always been there. In Lacanian terms, laughter would make a 'discovery' about the subject, finding out that they had always had the potential to laugh. By contrast, the claim 'I can laugh' does not provide sufficient evidence for the claim that Kakfa can laugh, a fact that recalls Freud comparison between objections/judgments and jokes where jokes come with the 'evidence' of laughter whereas claims do not. The claim 'I can laugh' in fact makes the

[56] For the example itself I must make special thanks to Anca Parvulescu, who read this brilliant letter of Kafka's to me during a paper in 2011 and whose work has always been the greatest of inspirations. I would like to point directly to her more recent article on the letter and on laughter in Kafka as well, which can be found here: Anca Paruvulescu, 'Kafka's Laughter: On Joy and the Kafkaesque', *PMLA*, vol. 130, no. 5 (October 2015), pp. 1420–32.

[57] Note that the letter is not reprinted in full here.

[58] Franz Kafka, *Letters to Felice*, ed. Erich Heller and Jurgen Born, trans. James Stern and Elizabeth Duckworth (New York: Schocken Boks, 1973), p. 200.

'evidence' which follows, the fact that other people consider him a 'great laugher', to be at least doubtful (Kafka even acknowledges Felice's possible doubt at his claim and tries to counter it, saying 'have no doubt about this'). Thus, it shows not only that laughter functions as an event that would turn Kakfa into a 'laugher' who has always had the potentiality to laugh but also that this event of laughter may easily not happen, humorously showing how the realities laughter brings into being cannot be thought of as inevitable. On the contrary, laughter can only arise in a certain set of conditions, as the letter goes on to explore.

Kafka's anxiety to be seen as a 'laugher' may because he thinks one must have the flexibility to laugh, to be open to its evental capacities for change, which are perhaps even present if the laughter is the self-affirming Hobbesian kind. For Kafka to claim that he *can* laugh is to imply that another *cannot*, and may recall eighteenth-century ideas of laughter as a sign of weakness (but which we can now read as a desire to be inflexible and secure). The Englishman Phillip Stanhope (1694–1793), who was the Fourth Earl of Chesterfield, is well known in English literary history as a figure who reportedly never laughed. In a letter to his son, he once wrote:

> I would heartily wish that you may often be seen to smile, but never heard to laugh while you live. Frequent and loud laughter is the characteristic of folly and ill-manners; it is the manner in which the mob express their silly joy at silly things; and they call it being merry. In my mind there is nothing so illiberal, and so ill-bred, as audible laughter. I am neither of a melancholy nor a cynical disposition, and am as willing and as apt to be pleased as anybody; but I am sure that since I have had the full use of my reason nobody has ever heard me laugh.[59]

The figure of Stanhope was humorously recreated by Charles Dickens in the character of Sir John Chester in the strangely understudied 1841 novel *Barnaby Rudge*. In that novel Chester, in exactly this kind attempt to maintain stable identity by protecting himself from the *evental* capacities of comedy, never laughs:

> The nearest approach to a laugh in which he ever indulged (and that but seldom and only on extreme occasions), never even curled his lip or effected the smallest change in – no, not so much as a slight wagging of – his great, fat, double chin, which at these times, as at all others,

[59] Phillip Dormer Stanhope, *Letters Written by the Earl of Chesterfield to His Son* (New York: Derby and Jackson, 1897), p. 149.

> remained a perfect desert in the broad map of his face; one changeless, dull, tremendous blank.[60]

It is Dickens's use of the world 'changeless' that points us to an important point about laughter's evental power. The fictional Sir Chester as Stanhope knows that to laugh would be to embrace a change in identity. Dickens makes writer and reader 'laughers' here by using a comic narrative style to recall 'the slight wagging of his great, fat, double chin', creating a distance between 'laughers' and 'non-laughers' (here 'non-laughers' are made the *object* of laughter) and establishing new identities through this comedy, enacting the very change that Stanhope wants to resist. Kafka's claim seems also to be grounded in this kind of realization about what laughter can do. His remark that 'in this respect I used to be far crazier than I am now' also seems to point towards laughter as a marker of change in subjectivity, and recalls discussions of laughter as disorder (see Chapter 2). Kafka's gesture to his lover seems to be that of saying 'don't think I am too inflexible, because I can laugh, but don't think I am too unstable either, I'm not like I used to be!' Kafka's letter goes on:

> It even happened to me once, at a solemn meeting with our president – it was two years ago, but the story will outlive me at the office – that I started to laugh, and how! It would be too involved to describe to you this man's importance; but believe me, it is very great: an ordinary employee thinks of this man as not on this earth, but in the clouds. And as we usually have little opportunity of talking to the Emperor, contact with this man is, for the average clerk – a situation common of course to all large organizations – tantamount to meeting the Emperor.[61]

By virtue of being about laughing in the wrong place the episode seems to recall ideas of laughter as arising from incongruity (Chapter 1) and it also seems to be about laughter's capacity to destroy structures of hierarchy, evoking the 'carnival' (Chapter 2). In framing the company boss as Emperor the passage is already humorous before any punchline, with Kafka's comic narration working against the emperor-like performance of the employer and anticipating the next:

> Needless to say, like anyone exposed to clear and general scrutiny whose position does not quite correspond to his achievements, this man invites ridicule; but to allow oneself to be carried away by laughter at something

[60] Charles Dickens, *Barnaby Rudge*, ed. John Bowen (London: Penguin, 2003), pp. 242–3.
[61] Kafka, *Letters to Felice*, p. 201.

> so commonplace and, what's more, in the presence of the great man himself, one must be out of one's mind.[62]

But these jokes about the boss and the non-correspondence of his achievements and persona do not serve simply to bring down the high and mighty to the basic human level. As discussed earlier, Zupančič works against the traditional argument that comedy brings the ideal down to the material, or the high down to the low, that comedy brings down ideology, affirming a basic human state underneath it all as if laughter is some kind of equalizing force. Opposing the idea that comedy 'shows that we are *only human*', she suggests that comedy can be a process that makes us appear to be more than material human. Similarly, Kakfa's comic world is not one in which everyone is an equal material human but one in which the 'ordinary employee thinks of [his boss] as not on this earth, but in the clouds', as of palpable spiritual significance. The humour of Kafka's letter shows something like Zupančič's argument. Certainly, his laughter does not operate to bring down appearances and show that we are all equals. Instead, his humour is found in showing how real these appearances are.

As the letter continues the laughter becomes evental, at least insofar as the event is 'that which exceeds its causes':

> At first I laughed only at the president's occasional delicate little jokes; but while it is a rule only to contort one's features respectfully at these little jokes, I was already laughing out loud . . .
>
> And now that I was in full spate, I was of course laughing not only at the current jokes, but at those of the past and the future and the whole lot together, and by then no one knew what I was really laughing about . . .
>
> The semblance of the world which hitherto I had seen before me dissolved completely, and I burst into loud and uninhibited laughter of such heartiness as perhaps only schoolchildren at their desks are capable of.[63]

As Anca Parvulescu has argued, at this moment the laughter appears to be something that we can think of in Bataillian or Deleuzian terms: a completely shattering event which resists rationalization.[64] In the moment of laughter, chronology appears blurred and time itself is temporarily suspended. Kafka writes, 'I was of course laughing not only at the current jokes, but at those of

62 Ibid.
63 Ibid.
64 Anca Parvulescu, 'Kafka's Laughter: On Joy and the Kafkaesque', PMLA, vol. 130, no. 5 (October 2015), pp. 1420–32.

the past and the future and the whole lot together.' It is as if, for the moment of laughter itself, time is broken and chronology is lost, the sense of cause and effect broken, with laughter something that cannot be seen as a response to anything visible and articulable at this moment. Perhaps it is after laughing that chronology is restored, or a new chronology is created.

Kafka makes attempts at rationalization, that that endless search for a cause that all laughter seems to ask for, but laughter again refuses to be seen as an effect of a cause:

> I produced innumerable excuses for my behavior, all of which might have been very convincing had not the renewed outbursts of laughter rendered them completely unintelligible.[65]

The president, 'born with an instinct for smoothing things out', joins in the quest to locate the cause of laughter, asking that age-old question of why we laugh.

> The president ... found some phrase that offered some reasonable explanation for my howls – I think an allusion to a joke he had made a long time before. He then hastily dismissed us. Undefeated, roaring with laughter yet desperately unhappy, I was the first to stagger out of the hall.[66]

The search for a cause for the laughter appears to fail, with the president's attempt to link the laughter to a former joke obviously a fairly weak explanation designed to 'smooth things over'. And yet, the last line of Kafka's letter shows his sense of laughter as an event which not only exceeds its causes but retroactively changes them. He finishes:

> I may have behaved in this fashion at the time simply in order to prove to you later that I am capable of laughter.[67]

This last line frames the whole letter as a joke, an attempted piece of proof of the statement 'I can laugh, Felice'. One single laugh would be proof enough, but in its place is an exposition many pages long detailing a reported experience of laughter which provides evidence for the validity of the initial claim. The laughter it recounts looks forward into its own unknown future,

[65] Kafka, *Letters to Felice*, p. 202.
[66] Ibid.
[67] Ibid.

in which is found its true cause, absent at the time of laughter. At the time, no one present can work out why the peals of laughter are issued, but its causes are open to retroactive change in the future. Laughter is never left without a cause but its causes can be retroactively and eventally changed, something Kakfa forces us to consider with the claim that the laughter occurs 'simply in order to prove to you later that I am capable of laughter', attempting to retroactively transform Kakfa into 'the great laugher' of the letter's opening. It also points to the evental retroactivity in all laughter.

If a simple laugh would have served the purpose of the whole letter, (the claim, the evidence and the conclusion in one), can we not say that the letter itself is symbolic of a laugh, and that every laugh functions exactly as this letter does? It makes a claim, and then provides evidence for this claim, before asserting that this effect of laughter demonstrates the truth of something that existed prior to the laugh, in this case Kafka's existing capacity to laugh. In this case the claim is simply 'I can laugh', for which laughter would of course be the evidence. But in the case of another laughter, that of superiority perhaps, or that of release, would the situation be any different? Such laughter can be thought of as the subject's claim to be superior, with the laughter issued proof of this superiority, and the construction of the appearance that the superiority always existed to be merely reflected and evidenced by the *effect* of laughter. In another case laughter might be the subject's claim to be free and liberated, with the event of laughter again proof of the subject's free and liberated experience, making it seem as if the subject always existed to be freed.

What the final part of the letter demonstrates is the properly evental function of laughter, which leaves the anxious residue found at the end of each laugh. It is the remainder in laughter in which, to use the words of Jean-Luc Nancy discussed earlier, sense or order *senses itself coming into being*. Laughter eventally brings the subject into a new structure of order, creating in its tiny moment a full argument, evidence and conclusion, and bringing the subject into this newly ordered reality which, it appears, cannot be contested: the evidence for its pre-existence is already provided by the laughter itself. And yet if laughter brings us into this new reality it also contains a signal from whence it came, showing that our apparently secure reality is in fact constructed by 'caesural' and 'evental' breaks. It is this 'signal' which accounts for the anxious qualities of laughter, the subject of the next chapter.

4

Laughter and Anxiety

Inside and outside of psychoanalysis, laughter has often been thought of as relating to anxiety and the idea of nervous laughter has been known since Hippocrates. The usual line about the relationship is that laughter can be a response to anxiety or a way of dealing with it: sometimes we laugh in situations we feel anxious to get out of or when we want to avoid confronting our anxieties. This chapter argues that laughter cannot be said to eradicate or 'deal with' anxiety and that laughter is always unsettling precisely because it contains anxiety and indicates its continuing threat. The chapter continues the earlier argument, discussing Freud and Lacan on anxiety, as well as Charles Mauron, an understudied writer whose *Psychocritique du Genre Comique*, written in 1964 and as yet not available in English, was the only sustained study of psychoanalysis and comedy to be written until Zupančič's 2008 *The Odd One In*.[1] I argue here that Mauron's idea of *renversement* holds a key to understanding the relationship between laughter and anxiety. In the second half of the chapter I provide a more sustained discussion of these ideas in relation to Nicolai Gogol's short story 'The Overcoat', a unique comic text that deals directly with the relationship between laughter and anxiety. Ultimately I want to show that the argument of this book, that laughter should be seen as an event, offers a framework for working through the difficult relationship between laughter and anxiety.

The central figure for discussions of anxiety is of course Freud, who first treated the subject in 1895 in a paper on neurosis. Freud's groundbreaking concepts of wit, and humour should also be mentioned, though he does not explicitly connect them to anxiety (*SE 7*: 1–247). Implicitly, this chapter is a step away from Freud's more 'heroic' interpretation of laughter and humour as liberation from the tensions and vicissitudes of life that were discussed in Chapter 1 and a move towards reading laughter in light of psychoanalytic anxiety. In his paper on neurosis Freud summarized his argument by writing that 'the mechanism of anxiety is to be looked for in a deflection of somatic sexual excitation from the physical sphere, and in a consequent abnormal

[1] Charles Mauron, *Psychocritque du Genre Comique* (Paris: Libraire Jose Corti, 1964).

employment of that excitation' (*SE 3*: 108). The claim here is that anxiety is a response to a more primary process which finds its way out of the unconscious in the transformed shape of anxiety. In other words, anxiety is caused by a non-normative interruption to the subject's development. Freud followed this initial idea that anxiety is the result of a blockage of some kind for some time, remarking in *The Interpretation of Dreams* that 'anxiety is a libidinal impulse which has its origin in the unconscious and is *inhibited* by the preconscious' (*SE 4*: 337–8, emphasis added). Likewise, in 1920 Freud wrote in the *Three Essays on Sexuality* that 'anxiety arises out of the libido, that it is a transformation of it' (*SE 7*: 224). The argument maintains the primacy of the sexual and places anxiety in the category of response or symptom. Indeed, Strachey notes that at this stage Freud was treating anxiety as purely physical, without any psychological determinants.[2]

However, as so often with Freud, and just like with his discussions of laughter, the initial explanation is elsewhere problematized within the body his own work. In a letter to Fliess as early as 1897 Freud had written that he had 'decided henceforth to regard as separate factors what causes libido and what causes anxiety', suggesting that he already considered the view of anxiety as response or symptom to be problematic.[3] In the 1926 *Inhibitions, Symptoms and Anxiety*, Freud's initial argument about anxiety is turned fully on its head; rather than seeing anxiety as a response to other factors, anxiety itself takes up a position as *primal*. From this point, Freud begins to think about what anxiety causes, rather than what it is caused *by*.

In the essay Freud demonstrates that anxiety cannot be seen as an anxiety *of* something, opposing anxiety to 'fear' or 'phobia'. A phobia, Freud says, is formed as a response to an undirected and unexplainable more primary anxiety. The phobia has two effects. First, it 'avoids conflict due to ambivalence' by centring unplaced anxiety around an object (*SE 20*: 125). Through this process 'an internal, instinctual danger' (that of unplaced anxiety) is replaced by an 'external, perceptual one' (that of fear directed at a particular object) (*SE 20*: 126). The second effect of the phobia is that 'it enables the ego to cease generating anxiety' (*SE 20*: 125). So, unlike fear, anxiety pre-exists: the ego is constantly generating anxiety until some action is taken to stop it; anxiety is seen here as the cause of repression rather than its result. Derrida picks up on the reversal, writing 'linked to repression, [anxiety] appears at first to be an effect, but later, in *Inhibition, Symptom and Anxiety* Freud will say,

2 For details of this, see James Strachey's introduction to *Inhibitions, Symptoms and Anxiety* in *SE* 20: 78–9.

3 See Jeffrey Moussaieff Masson (ed.), *The Complete Letters of Sigmund Freud to Wilhelm Fleiss* (Cambridge, MA: Belknap Press, 1986).

à propos of Little Hans, that anxiety *produces* repression' (my emphasis).[4] Rather than being a transformed or repressed version of something more primary, in this reading anxiety comes first, and is controlled and repressed via symbolic organization which transforms it into fear. In other words, we can say that for Freud, fear is anxiety after it has been given an object. When we become scared *of* something repression has occurred and anxiety can cease generating. The argument made here is that laughter is also involved in this process; laughter gives anxiety an 'object', or at least attempts to.

In his seminar on anxiety (1962–3) Lacan picks up on the Freud of *Inhibitions, Symptoms and Anxiety*. He describes anxiety as an affect, and qualifies this by specifying that an 'affect is not repressed, and this is something that Freud says just like me'. The affect, for Lacan, is 'unmoored', it 'goes with the drift' 'displaced, mad, inverted, but not repressed'. The subject experiences anxiety as something which is not held in check by forces of repression. What is repressed, Lacan continues 'are the signifiers that moor it'; when anxiety begins to be dealt with, directed and ordered, repression is in play (*S10*: 11). As it is for the Freud of *Inhibitions, Symptoms and Anxiety*, for Lacan the affect of anxiety is in some way primal, or originary to the subject, rather than the result of something impeding its development. Anxiety is the cause of repression because it forces the subject to organize and direct this anxiety onto an object, changing anxiety into, for instance, fear.

In another turn of the screw, Lacan reverses Freud's theory of anxiety to state that in fact we are always afraid 'of' something, that anxiety 'is not without an object' (*S10*: 77). However, the subject 'does not know what object is involved' (*S10*: 77). This 'something' that the subject is afraid of is not an articulable object, it is not in the realm of the symbolic, it is 'an object which is outside any possible definition of objectivity' (*S10*: 75). In *Ethics of the Real*, Alenka Zupančič uses a joke to develop this Lacanian idea:

> A patient comes to [his analyst] complaining that a crocodile is hiding under his bed. During several sessions the analyst tries to persuade the patient that this is all in his imagination. A month later the analyst meets a friend, who is also a friend of his ex-patient, and asks him how the latter is. The friend answers: 'Do you mean the one who was eaten by a crocodile?' The lesson of this story is profoundly Lacanian; if we start from the idea that anxiety does not have an object, what are we then to call this thing which killed, which 'ate' the subject? What is the subject

[4] Jacques Derrida, *The Postcard: From Socrates to Freud and Beyond* (London: University of Chicago Press, 1987), p. 297.

> telling the analyst in this joke? Nothing other than: 'I have the *objet petit a* under my bed; I came too close to it.'[5]

The introduction of the *objet petit a* allows for an understanding of anxiety which holds that it simultaneously *has* and *does not have* an object. The object of anxiety is the *objet petit a*. This difficult concept can be thought of as the inaccessible or the object beyond the subject. In Lacan's work, from the seminar on anxiety onwards, the *objet a* comes to denote the object which can never be attained, which is the cause of desire rather than that towards which desire tends.[6] In this sense it is to be seen as an 'objective' as well as an 'object'; it is that which the subject desires, and that which the subject desires to be, both the object of desire, and the object-cause of desire: that which sets desire on its course. Anxiety must be thought of alongside desire, and indeed Lacan calls anxiety 'the sign of desire', since both anxiety and desire can be seen as without an articulable object. Both anxiety and desire are unplaced and infinite, but then become 'moored' by being given a symbolic object.

Explaining the *objet a* in greater detail Lacan relates the concept to the foundational idea of the mirror stage. In his early mirror stage essay, Lacan establishes the formation of the subject as the taking on of the 'armour of an alienating identity'.[7] Here, the subject (mis)recognises itself as a whole in the mirror, and simultaneously perceives its own inadequacy in relation to this supposed unified image which it sees, thereby constituting the subject by lack; its first sense of itself as subject is in relation to its failure to live up to its image. Its image, or its identity, becomes its armour, but it is also that which alienates the subject since the subject appears to be lacking a completeness which the image possesses. This lack is the cause of anxiety, but it is also the object-cause of desire, since it appears as the object which would complete the subject, the *objet petit a*. In Seminar 11 Lacan explains that 'the *objet a* is something from which the subject, in order to constitute itself, has separated itself off as organ. This serves as the symbol of lack, that is to say, of the phallus, not as such, but in so far as it is lacking' (*S11*: 103). Any particular object which the subject later organizes its desire around is a false appearance of desire, which deals with the more originary and unplaced desire by anchoring this lack to an object that the subject does not possess. Lacan remarks that 'objects prior to the status of the common object are … what is involved in the *objet a*' (*S10*: 80). The unknown object around which

5 Alenka Zupančič, *Ethics of the Real: Kant and Lacan* (London: Verso, 2011), p. 145.
6 For the development of the term in Lacan, see Dylan Evans, *An Introductory Dictionary of Lacanian Terms* (London: Routledge, 1996), p. 125.
7 Jacques Lacan, *Ecrits: A Selection*, trans. Alan Sheridan (London: Routledge, 1989), p. 78.

the subject structures itself then determines 'communicable' objects; actual objects, objects of everyday life. What is important here is the relationship between this unplaced desire and anxiety. Anxiety is the counterpart of the *objet a* because it expresses the undirected affect that the subject experiences prior to organizing itself by 'mooring' this unplaced experience around designated objects. Anxiety, considered as a desire (before those directed desires), is both anticipation and prevention, longing and dread. Interestingly *OED* confirms this, retaining both 'desire' and 'uneasiness' as meanings. Common talk also reflects this doubleness; anxiety is a desire for something and a desire to avoid something, as with the phrase 'I am anxious to meet him'/'I am anxious not to meet him'. Anxiety needs to be translated into something with an object, whether that be an object to fear or an object to desire.

In Lacan's formulation, from the point of view of anxiety, fear and desire are undifferentiated, they have not been 'determined'. Fear *of* and desire *for* are closely connected because both are produced as a response to anxiety, which operates as a kind of turning point in the subject's development. As we shall see, laughter is a process which *gives anxiety an object*; it can be thought of as the movement which takes the subject from unplaced and unmoored anxiety to a rational structure in which there is a clear object, whether that be an object of fear, desire or laughter. It is in this sense that laughter might be said to 'deal with' anxiety, but it does not remove anxiety since it also contains a dangerous 'signal' of the anxiety from which it came.

Psychoanalyst Charles Mauron links laughter to anxiety in his 1964 book *La Psychocritique du Genre Comique*, one of the few sustained studies of psychoanalysis and comedy.[8] As this book has attempted to establish, there is a fruitful relationship between psychoanalysis and laughter since psychoanalysis can be thought of as an investigation into how the subject comes into being and laughter plays a unique role in the formation of subjects, and it seems Mauron was the first to significantly explore the link. Mauron remarks that comedy is 'la *renversement* des situations d'angoisse', (the reversal of the situation of anxiety).[9] Mauron's argument develops to see comedy as a safety mechanism for dealing with anxiety. He argues that comedy provides a release from psychic blockage, so that it deals with and solves psychic problems. As such, he ultimately comes down on the side of those who have tended to see laughter as 'liberating'. There is a parallel between Mauron and Northrop Frye's more obviously conventional

[8] For a very important discussion of Mauron, see Jonathan Hall, *Anxious Pleasures*, (London: Associated University Press, 1995).

[9] Mauron, *Psychocritque du Genre Comique*, p. 72.

comments on comedy. Frye remarks that 'psychologically [comedy] is like the removal of a neurosis or blocking point and the restoration of an unbroken current of energy'.[10] Mauron belongs with those psychoanalysts, unlike Lacanians, who place the ego at the centre, seeing the protection of the ego as something we ought to achieve. In this reading comedy is a successful process on the side of the ego that deals with anxiety, removing it. But while Mauron's belief in protecting and serving the ego might be open to critique, he hits on something important about the link between laughter and anxiety here: that laughter is a partially successful *attempt* to give anxiety an object.

That Mauron should describe the process of moving from anxiety to comedy as 'renversement' is more than suggestive. Renversement implies inverting or reverting one thing into something else, and *OED* retains a sense that renversement has been historically used as a synonym for metamorphosis, making it not so very far from ideas of event. While Mauron elsewhere claims that laughter helps the subject grow and develop, 'renversement' does not imply progress or development but a strange movement both forwards and back. Thus, if laughter is related to anxiety it is not straightforwardly as a progress from it or a 'dealing with' it. Rather, it implies 'inversing' anxiety, which means both reversing and transferring, perhaps trying to deal with it but also keeping anxiety within it or returning to it.

On the other hand, it may be the case that we can never quite know if and when an event has taken place. One critic who comes close to seeing laughter as eventual is Shane Weller, who associates laughter in Baudelaire and in Samuel Beckett with the idea of 'the end'. Via Baudelaire, Weller writes:

> Who laughs? At whom or at what do they laugh? And to what end? Baudelaire's response is that only the unknowing self can laugh, that it can laugh only at the self mistaken for the other, and that the end of laughter is the wisdom that does not laugh. As for the last laugh, however, this is not a laugh at the other but the laugh of the other, a laugh that is produced only in that liminal space of knowing-unknowing, of apparent unknowing, or, more precisely, of unknowing's appearance, for which Baudelaire's name is art.[11]

The conception is relevant to what has been argued here. Laughter may be an event that must remain partially unknowable, or to take place in the liminal space between knowing and unknowing, at least to those in whom

[10] Frye, *Anatomy of Criticism*, p. 171.
[11] Shane Weller, *Beckett, Literature and the Ethics of Alterity* (London: Palgrave Macmillan, 2006), p. 88.

the event has occurred. It may be that the events transformative power is retrospectively visible only from outside.

Another connection between Weller's reading and the idea of evental laughter is the suggestion that laughter is a movement that is neither forward nor backward. Following Beckett's comedy, Weller argues that 'any movement 'on' will inevitably encounter its own knowable impossibility' and laughter may be thought of as such a movement 'on'.[12] This Beckettian movement 'on' is without implications of progress and comes from the opening line of his prose play *Worstward Ho!*, which puns on Kingsley's 1855 *Westward Ho!*, criticizing the idea of moving in a positive forward direction. The opening reads:

> On. Say on. Be said on. Somehow on. Till nohow on. Said nohow on.

The line combines humour with movement but rejects movement forward by punning on 'no'. While the dominant ideas of laughter as liberating, controlling or as a way of dealing with anxiety all often conceive of laughter as a movement of progress or regression, evental laughter does not have this linear implication. This would be another link between the event and Mauron's concept of renversement.

Interestingly, Mauron reads Thomas Hobbes against the grain, arguing that there is an inward dialectical movement in the subject, overturning earlier commentators who see Hobbes's thesis as evidence of the static and ahistorical ideology of hierarchical superiority and/or moral censure. For Hobbes the 'sudden glory' we experience when we erupt into laughter may be evidence of our confidence and security, just as for Bergson, who writes that the comic cannot produce the effect of laughter unless it falls 'on the surface of a soul that is thoroughly calm and unruffled'.[13] On the contrary, Mauron works with the notion of the self's illusory superiority, which is only momentarily sustained against the perception of its own weakness and inferiority. Thus, if we laugh to assert superiority what we are dealing with is not so much an assertion of existing superiority but the creation of superiority or a weak attempt to sustain it. Seen in this way, laughter risks revealing that there is nothing behind it the superiority it establishes or at least showing how fragile those structures of superiority are.[14] It may be that

[12] Ibid., p. 194.

[13] Bergson, *Laughter*, p. 10.

[14] Michael Billig similarly sees Hobbes as a writer concerned with self-deception; see his *Laughter and Ridicule: Towards a Social Critique of Humour* (London: Sage, 2005), p. 55.

laughter is an assertion of our unruffledness, but it is assertion with anxiety within it that indicates how ruffled we really are.

This could be placed in the context of Aristotle's comments on comedy, which are more complex than is often thought. Used earlier as an example of 'superiority theory' in which laughter is provoked by something 'ugly', a closer reading shows another dimension to Aristotle's conception. In *Poetics* he writes that

> Comedy is, as we said, a representation of people who are rather inferior – not, however, with respect to every kind of vice, but the laughable is only a part of what is ugly. For the laughable is a sort of error and ugliness that is not painful and destructive, just as, evidently, a laughable mask is something ugly and distorted without pain.[15]

Thus, the ethical function of comedy is distinct from condemnation. For Aristotle, Comedy and Tragedy descend genealogically from invective or cursing and hymns respectively, where one is a song of praise for heroes and the other a harsh condemnation of enemies. Yet, he explains in this passage that the apparently moral distinction between the noble and ignoble is displaced since in comedy we have ridicule without moral condemnation, error and ugliness without pain and suffering. While the more traditional superiority theory would be an example of giving anxiety an object (the ugly or inferior target), associating laughter with cruelty, the idea of laughter as 'error' or as ugliness itself (rather than as a response to ugliness) suggests a connection between laughter and anxiety instead. It may be that laughter is a misattempt at superiority, a moment which brings the laughing subject into being via a failed assertion of themselves vis-à-vis the target. It may also be that in dramatizing the attempt to give anxiety an object, comedy leaves the object in tact but shows the subject in an anxious position of self-assertion.

Such a point can be considered in relation to a wider Freudian terminology of anxiety, fear and cathexis. Cathexis is a psychoanalytic term describing the concentration of mental energy on one particular person, idea, or object, so laughter can be seen – from a certain perspective at least – as a cathecting process. Of cathexis, Todd McGowan writes that through a 'process of symbolization, we do away with the need for continued repression', creating a situation in which 'the unconscious no longer speaks, where once it was open, now it is closed'.[16] For McGowan, 'symbolization always silences the

[15] Aristotle, 'Poetics', in *The Norton Anthology of Theory and Criticism*, ed. Vincent B. Leitch (London: W. W. Norton, 2001), pp. 88–115 (p. 92).

[16] Todd McGowan, *The Feminine 'No!': Psychoanalysis and the New Canon* (Albany: SUNY Press, 2001), p. 21.

unconscious', and we may be able to put laughter in these terms as well. By attempting to translate unconscious anxiety into a state of conscious fear via a process of cathexis, laughter tries to silence the unconscious. What Lacan adds to the Freudian model is the continued presence of excess – or *jouissance* – in such a moment. There is an excessive *jouissance* that escapes symbolization even in this moment of 'conservative' preservation which leaves anxiety present and threatening. This gives laughter its subversive edge in the very moment of an attempt to preserve or assert the subject. This dialectical feature of laughter, at once subject preserving and simultaneously excessive, makes psychoanalysis a vital tool for its understanding.

This speaks to the idea of the 'event' as developed via Badiou. Insofar as the event is that which exceeds its causes it is also that which contains an excess that escapes symbolization, showing the particular importance of psychoanalysis in the concept. While the cathexis that translates anxiety into fear is on the conservative side of ideology, this excess – definitional of the event – is its simultaneously present subversive underside. Further, my focus in discussing the event has been to show its power to disrupt models of chronological time and I have tried to show how laughter contains this peculiar potential. Since the event exceeds its causes, it destabilizes the narrative it erupts into, bring past, present and future into a new connection. It may 'deal with' anxiety by creating a new narrative, but it also threatens and destabilizes the narrative it creates by showing it to be just that: a material creation.

These discussions of anxiety have provided two hypotheses. The first is that laughter and anxiety share a number of characteristics, and that laughter is in a certain sense borne out of anxiety. In this role *laughter functions to give anxiety an object*. Second, it has been argued that laughter does not eradicate anxiety but always contains the 'signal' of the anxiety from which it comes. In line with the idea of laughter as an event, if laughter produces a kind of symbolic order and apparently secure structure in which there are designated objects for our anxieties, then it also shows this process happening to the subject, signalling the anxiety that is foundational to subjectivity. Both of these things can be seen in Gogol's short story 'The Overcoat', which I will now use as my final extended example.

Gogol's Overcoat, laughter's objects

'The Overcoat' is a short comedy about anxiety and, even more specifically, about the relationship between anxiety and laughter. It seems to be this exact relationship that Gogol sets out to explore from the beginning of the text. This marks Gogol out from later authors in the Russian tradition. Nikos Kazantzakis, for example, who was strongly influenced by Bergson, whose lectures he attended in Paris in 1907–8, remarked in his 1952 novel *Zorba the Greek* that laughter is a salvation given only to the courageous, not to anxious men, following Bergson's idea that laughter is the act of the 'unruffled'.

The story is set in the tightly wound and anxious community of 'a certain Russian ministerial department' and recounts the experiences of Akaki Akakievitch, an office clerk who enjoys his role as part of the infinite bureaucracy that Gogol's work so often pokes fun at. It seems that the comedy of the character comes from the fact that he lacks any individuality or uniqueness. Still, Akaki is very different from his environment, which is strongly emphasized by the narrator. The narrator is essential for the understanding of Gogol's text and the interplay between anxiety and laughter. Notably, the narrator evokes much of the laughter in the story; he laughs at his characters, he is full of irony, but also of compassion. The narrator reveals the absurdity of Akaki's world thus provoking feelings other than laughter, too. As Gogol's friend Pushkin said, we could see Gogol's invisible tears behind his visible laughter.[17] Yet, despite his compassion, via the narrator Gogol disperses the anxiety, laughs at the world and even at his readers, thus turning anxiety on the level of his interaction with the reader into freedom. It is necessary to acknowledge the narrator's presence and functions in connection to the hypotheses developed in this paper about the link between laughter and anxiety.

Akakievitch seems comically to be something of a surface creature, as if an 'extra' in a television show, rather than a complete human with full subjectivity.

> He was always seen in the same spot, in the same attitude, busy with the same work, and bearing the same title; so that people began to believe he had come into the world just as he was, with his bald forehead and official uniform.[18]

Part of the backdrop, Akaki Akakievitch (a name with the comic value of John Johnson) appears merely a 'character type'. Character typing in comedy probably began with the creation of Roman New Comedy. As discussed

[17] Discussed in J. H. Billington, *The Icon and the Axe: An Interpretive History of Russian Culture* (New York: Vintage Books, 1970).

[18] Nikolai Gogol, *The Collected Tales of Nikolai Gogol* (Vintage: New York, 1999), pp. 394–424 (p. 395).

earlier, while the Old Comedy of Aristophanes (Hegel's prime example of comedy) is characterized by exaggerated laughter, the sexual and the erotic, in New Comedy these characteristics are notably absent. As Leo Salingar discussed, the fantastic puns and metaphors of Old Comedy disappear along with lampooning, obscenity and exaggerated stage phalluses. Indeed, even Roman critics praised New Comedy for its well-made plots and insight into 'character types' that were 'true to life'.[19] The framework of Old and New Comedy is useful again here in discussing the comedy of character types. While Old Comedy seemed to involve a celebration of freedom, making it a laughter that 'liberates', New Comedy was about how restricted and controlled individuals were by their social roles, a controlling comedy that showed how restricted and mechanical we are. It suggests that there is not much to the man beyond his social construction, challenging ideas of unique individuality and making humans merely repeating machines.

In 'The Overcoat' Akakievitch is specifically described as a mechanical being, recalling Henri Bergson's famous suggestion that laughter is caused by the perception of 'something mechanical encrusted on the living':[20]

> Outside this copying nothing appeared to exist for him. He did not even think of his clothes. His uniform, which was originally green, had acquired a reddish tint. The collar was so narrow and so tight that his neck, although of average length, stretched far out of it, and appeared extraordinarily long, just like those of the cats with movable heads, which are carried about on trays and sold to the peasants in Russian villages.[21]

The repetition is important and connects Bergson to Freud via comedy. The repetition has to do with Freudian 'mastery' and Gogol's character never makes a mistake in his copying because he has completely mastered his repetitious job. The repetition becomes machinic and contains a frightening reminder that identity is produced by repetitious structures (which may be a point hidden beneath the surface of Bergson's claim too).

Typically the laughter found *in* New Comedy, not to be confused with the potential laughter produced in the shows audience, was based on mocking, tricking, humiliating and embarrassing. It is a laughter directed *at* an individual, not a laughter that subsumes the stage, engulfing all in a heterogeneous chaos. It can therefore be seen as a laughter of superiority,

[19] Gilbert Norwood, *Greek Comedy* (London: Methuen, 1931), pp. 314–17.
[20] See Bergson, *Laughter*, p. 34.
[21] Gogol, *The Collected Tales of Nikolai Gogol*, p. 398.

re-enforcing existing social value systems and codes. The same laughter is found *in* 'The Overcoat', and again should be contrasted with the potential laughter the story can provoke in the reader. The usual target for this laughter is Akakievitch:

> His young colleagues made him the butt of their ridicule and their elegant wit, so far as officials can be said to possess any wit. They did not scruple to relate in his presence various tales of their own invention regarding his manner of life and his landlady, who was seventy years old. They declared that she beat him, and inquired of him when he would lead her to the marriage altar. Sometimes they let a shower of scraps of paper fall on his head, and told him they were snowflakes.[22]

We might say that the world of the story is characterized by the laughter of Thomas Hobbes, where laughter provides a comforting assertion of superiority over another. While Akakievitch does not experience this kind of laughter himself, it characterizes the atmosphere of the story's setting in the 'Russian ministerial department':

> He never took any notice of what was going on in the streets, in contrast to his colleagues who were always watching people closely and whom nothing delighted more than to see someone walking along on the opposite pavement with a rent in his trousers.[23]

While the other characters of the story have self-affirming confidence and indulge in the laughter of superiority, Akakievitch is ridden with anxiety, finding it difficult even to speak to others. It is perhaps that these kinds of laughter, so common among the workers at the ministerial office, produce a target of laughter and establish an order that affirms one over another and keeps anxiety at bay. The atmosphere may still be one of 'fear' but it is not one of anxiety, since there is a known object and target at all times. It is this laughter which produces the kind of subjectivity found in the text, a kind of Hobbesian confident subject. Soren Kierkegaard's *The Concept of Anxiety*, an influence of Lacan, also discusses the distinction between fear and anxiety and Kierkegaard likewise writes that '[Anxiety] is altogether different from fear and similar concepts that refer to something definite.[24] While the

22 Ibid., p. 401.
23 Ibid.
24 Soren Kierkegaard, *The Concept of Anxiety*, ed. and trans. Reidar Thomte (Princeton: Princeton University Press, 1980). Lacan references Kierkegaard directly in *SX*: 15.

characters of 'The Overcoat' may be in fear (fear of losing their jobs, fear of becoming the object of ridicule themselves), they are not in the atmosphere of anxiety.

On the contrary, while the other characters have a Hobbesian confidence that holds anxiety at bay, Akakievitch is paralyzed to the point where he can barely articulate himself:

> 'I come just – merely – in order – I want –'
>
> We must here remark that the modest titular councillor was in the habit of expressing his thoughts only by prepositions, adverbs, or particles, which never yielded a distinct meaning. If the matter of which he spoke was a difficult one, he could never finish the sentence he had begun. So that when transacting business, he generally entangled himself in the formula 'Yes – it is indeed true that –' Then he would remain standing and forget what he wished to say, or believe that he had said it.[25]

It may even be that there is a resistance to subjectivity in Akakievitch's anxiety, since he avoids grammatical assertions of distinct meanings that assert any kind of subject-position, using only prepositions, particles and adverbs. Yet, this soon changes as Akakievitch begins to take on a subjectivity more like that of his colleagues. Akakievitch is speaking to a tailor here and is informed that he will need to purchase a new coat. The coat will be so expensive that Akakievitch will have to skip dinner, avoid using electricity and walk on the softest part of the pavement to make his shoes last longer, in order to afford this new coat. Yet, the quest for the coat appears to abate Akakievitch's anxiety and start him on the path to being more like his colleagues:

> At first he found these deprivations rather trying; but gradually he got accustomed to them, and at last took to going to bed without any supper at all. Although his body suffered from this abstinence, his spirit derived all the richer nutriment from perpetually thinking about his new cloak. From that time it seemed as though his nature had completed itself; as though he had married and possessed a companion on his life journey. This companion was the thought of his new cloak, properly wadded and lined.
>
> From that time he became more lively, and his character grew stronger, like that of a man who has set a goal before himself which he will reach at all costs. All that was indecisive and vague in his gait and

[25] Gogol, *The Collected Tales of Nikolai Gogol*, p. 403.

> gestures had disappeared. A new fire began to gleam in his eyes, and in his bold dreams he sometimes even proposed to himself the question whether he should not have a marten-fur collar made for his coat.[26]

It is clear to see that we are in the realms of Freudian anxiety, where the overcoat of the story's title provides an 'object' for anxiety, providing a 'goal' to strive towards and setting desire on its now clearly demarcated course. The coat even causes Akakievitch's gestures to lose their 'vague' and 'indecisive' qualities as his anxiety is hidden or apparently dealt with. The overcoat is the *objet a* discussed earlier, which appears as the object that will complete the subject but is also the object of desire in the sense of an *objective*, that which starts desire on its course: it is made clear that Akakievitch has had no desire to advance in the company or rise socially before the introduction of this coat. The introduction of the *objet a* produces a transformation which turns the mechanical and repetitious comic figure into the desiring modern subject with complete subjectivity structured around lack, in this case the humorous lack of the overcoat. The overcoat functions like Claudel's Pensee de Coufontaine in Lacan's discussion in his eighth seminar, a 'substitution for the *object a*' which itself remains unrepresentable (*S8*: 266). The 'narcissistic overvaluation' that Lacan describes there is also present in the figure of Akakievitch, who is transformed into the narcissistic subject with aspirations, even considering the class signifier of a 'marten-fun collar' for his new coat.

Anxiety though, is only held at bay until the coat is made by the tailor, at which point the threat of anxiety returns as the subject realizes desire is not fulfillable. Like the man eaten by the crocodile underneath his bed in the joke told by Zupančič, Akakivitch is destroyed by contact with the *objet a* of the overcoat.

> I do not know how the report spread in the office that Akaki's old cloak had ceased to exist. All his colleagues hastened to see his splendid new one, and then began to congratulate him so warmly that he at first had to smile with self-satisfaction, but finally began to feel embarrassed.[27]

Immediately his anxiety returns and his manners and gestures return to their previous stuttering form: 'he stammered out, blushing, that the cloak was not so new as it appeared; it was really second-hand'. Remaining the butt of his colleagues' jokes, Akakievitch continually suffers and eventually his coat is stolen, possibly by colleagues hounding and teasing him to extreme. Finally

[26] Ibid., p. 410.
[27] Ibid., p. 415.

he becomes ill and dies as a result of the cold (exacerbated by his missing coat) and the stress of having lost his beloved garment which took so much of his energy to acquire.

The tale then turns to the Superintendent, one of several figures in the story who have refused to help Akakievitch out in his time of need. The Superintendent is a man like those colleagues of Akakievitch discussed earlier, who jokes at the expense of others and revels in his own success. After Akakievitch's death he begins to sense the beginnings of anxiety and uses humour in an attempt to ward it off. The laughter of superiority that 'deals with' anxiety returns, but this time with a difference.

> At supper he drank two glasses of champagne, which, as everyone knows, is an effective means of heightening one's cheerfulness.
>
> As he sat in his sledge, wrapped in his mantle, on his way home, his mind was full of pleasant reveries. He thought of the society in which he had passed such a cheerful evening, and of all the excellent jokes with which he had made them laugh. He repeated some of them to himself half-aloud, and laughed at them again.[28]

The French translation of the story is 'Le Manteau', and the mantle he wears is an indication of the difference between him and Akakievitch. His humour is once more an attempt to ward off anxiety. But it seems less effective now, and he has to repeat the jokes to himself again and again as if to assure himself of the subject positions they established. Threatened by anxiety, the Superintendent attempts to use humour to re-establish his secure subjectivity:

> From time to time, however, he was disturbed in this cheerful mood by violent gusts of wind, which from some corner or other blew a quantity of snowflakes into his face, lifted the folds of his cloak, and made it belly like a sail, so that he had to exert all his strength to hold it firmly on his shoulders. Suddenly he felt a powerful hand seize him by the collar. He turned round, perceived a short man in an old, shabby uniform, and recognized with terror Akaki's face, which wore a deathly pallor and emaciation.[29]

But it is as if the world of 'The Overcoat' has moved from that of Hobbes to that of Mauron. Where before laughter provided a comfort to those laughing, seeming to reinforce their existing superiority, now laughter contains that

[28] Ibid., p. 422.
[29] Ibid., p. 423.

dangerous reminder that there is nothing behind the superiority it attempts to establish. This provides a nice illustration of Mauron's notion that laughter may work off the self's illusory superiority, which is only momentarily sustained against the perception of its own weakness and inferiority. After laughing, we are not only haunted by fear (the fear that we might have offended, that we might ourselves be laughed at), but by a less definitive and indefinable anxiety that we have failed to ward off. After the visitation by the ghost of anxiety, security of character is something of the past for the Superintendent:

> From that day onwards he no longer addressed to his subordinates in a violent tone the words, 'Do you know with whom you are speaking? Do you know who is standing before you?' Or if it ever did happen that he spoke to them in a domineering tone, it was not till he had first listened to what they had to say.[30]

Certainty of identity is lost as laughter reminds the 'laugher' of the primal anxiety on which subjectivity is founded. The whole of Gogol's story then, while it might appear to be set in the world of Thomas Hobbes, is rather more accurately the world of Charles Mauron's Hobbes against the grain. 'The Overcoat' is an explication on the laughter–anxiety relationship as *renversement*, a movement away from anxiety and a turn back to it. Akakievitch eventually comes to represent anxiety and operate as a ghost, a kind of return of repressed anxiety, not haunting the Superintendent again but returning to haunt 'various persons', including a sentinel who 'was of such a nervous disposition that he had been chaffed about his timidity more than once'. Anxiety is never 'dealt with' but always returns, threatening the stability of the subject at its foundations. Laughter may well be the attempt to ward off this anxiety by giving it an object, but it also contains a frightful reminder of it. This might go some way to explaining why laughter makes us to tired afterwards, because after laughter you can relax, with anxiety warded off, and also because energy has been expended coming close to anxiety and dealing with it.

To relate this to the idea of laughter as event, we can say that the two arguments run parallel to each other. The movement from anxiety to laughter, in Gogol and elsewhere, should be described as an *evental* movement. This event of laughter transforms anxiety into something else, perhaps turning it outwards and against others rather than inwards and onto the subject itself. The evental movement is an ideological one in which imposes order, holding

[30] Ibid.

at bay the threat of anxiety and the breakdown and disorder that comes with that threat. Laughter is therefore an event on the side of the subject, preserving it and protecting it. At the same time, however, this laughter seems to turn back to anxiety, so that the relationship between the two is best described as a *renversement*. This anxiety is not the same as the former but a new anxiety. The new anxiety comes from the fact that laughter, as a movement which constructs and protects the subject, serves as a frightful reminder that the subject was constructed and is therefore unsecure. In other words, because the subject is brought into being by events, these events themselves can also unsecure the subject, showing it to be something brought into being my moments such as this (such as laughter) and not something natural, pre-existing and secure.

Most importantly, this discussion of laughter and anxiety, I hope, provides an example of the kind of discussion that a theory of laughter as event can give rise to. It is not a simple illustration of that theory but an exploration of how the idea of laughter as event can offer a new framework for thinking about what comedy does. When laughter is seen eventally, it can open up new ways of discussing the various aspects of laughter and its functions. In this case the relationship between laughter and anxiety, a long-standing difficulty in laughter studies, has been at least somewhat illuminated by the theoretical framework of laughter as an event. This, I believe, is just one of many such relationships that could be put in terms of laughter and the event to produce useful analysis.

Conclusion

It would be extremely interesting to write a history of laughter.
Alexander Herzen/Mikhail Bakhtin[1]

Chaplin and fascism: Laughter's eventual evental interpretations

I have chosen to begin the conclusion of this book on comedy with a discussion of fascism. To be more specific, I want to address Theodor Adorno's famous comments about the comedy of Bertolt Brecht and Charlie Chaplin and how Adorno's criticism of a certain kind of comedy relates to the discussions in this book.

It is surprisingly unsurprising to talk about fascism and laughter together: the connection is the issue raised by much of Chaplin's comedy, as well as by many other comedians from Lubitsch to Mel Brooks, and it is an issue that has been ghosting the argument of this book. In what follows, by 'fascist laughter' I do not mean laughter which is necessarily about fascism or laughter that is necessarily issued by fascists, but laughter which could itself be described as structurally fascist. Provisionally, we can say that fascist laughter is any laughter which works by founding the identity of the person laughing by violently expelling and excluding the 'other'. To borrow the term famously coined by Julia Kristeva, we could say that such a laughter '*abjects*'.[2] Building on Lacan, Kristeva defines the abject as a reaction to a threatened breakdown in meaning caused by the loss of a clear distinction between subject and object or between self and other. So, the abject refers to a threat that meaning and identities are breaking down but also describes the affectual response the subject experiences when it encounters this threat. This chimes with the argument of the previous chapter, which argued that laughter gives anxiety an object, dealing with a threat, but also signalling

1 Bakhtin, *Rabelais and His World*, p. 59.
2 Jeannie B. Thomas has discussed laughter in terms of abjection in *Featherless Chicken, Laughing Women and Serious Stories* (Virginia: University of Virginia Press, 1997), p. 59.

the subject's fragility. In this sense laughter can be abjection in action, and this could be described as its 'fascist' quality, since it expels the other in an attempt to keep the subject secure or create secure identity.[3]

One clear example, from a definitively fascist context, is that of the Nazi 'mock museums'. The most famous of these was the Munich exhibition *Entartete Kunst* in 1937. These exhibitions, one exhibit of which was van Gogh's *Portrait of Dr Gachet*, functioned by turning threatening material with the potential to put fascism into question into objects of laughter and derision. This laughter expelled the other and secured the position of those laughing, banishing the anxiety initially provoked by the exhibits themselves. This example embodies the function of fascist laughter, which is not strictly the laughter of fascists but a laughter that emerges in a great many contexts: it is a laughter that creates a distance, establishing the identity of the 'laughers' by repelling another object.

In his essay 'Commitment', discussing Brecht's treatment of fascism, Adorno writes that both Chaplin and Brecht (the specific texts in question are *Arturo Ui* and *The Great Dictator*) are guilty of producing a comedy that trivializes fascism, making light of it and not showing us the truth about fascism (which is how close we are to being fascist ourselves), creating a kind of comedy that distances the viewer from the fascism that we laugh at. For Adorno these comedies hide us from the truly troubling reality: that fascism is an underlying structure that is dangerously close to that of our own social world. Instead, these comedies make it seem as though we – in the laughing West today – are far removed from the fascist world that we are laughing at when presented with a play by Brecht or a film by Chaplin. Adorno writes:

> Instead of a conspiracy of the wealthy and powerful, we are given a trivial gangster organization, the cabbage trust. The true horror of fascism is conjured away; it is no longer a slow end-product of the concentration of social power, but mere hazard, like an accident or crime.[4]

The language used is particularly important here. According to Adorno, in both Brecht and Chaplin's comedy, fascism is presented as a 'crime' or an 'accident', rather than as the 'slow end-product' of the ideology of our own 'wealthy and powerful', the eventual and evental end that our ideologically problematic society, for Adorno, is destined for. Thus, their comedy refuses to confront the fascism underlying our own ideology, the fact that if we carry

[3] See Julia Kristeva, *Powers of Horror: An Essay on Abjection*, trans. Leon S. Roudiez (New York: Columbia University Press, 1982), pp. 2–12.

[4] Theodor Adorno, 'Commitment', in *Aesthetics and Politics*, ed. Theodor Adorno et al. (London: Verso, 2007), pp. 177–96 (p. 184).

on as we are we will end up fascist, instead 'othering' it and forcing it to take on the status of either a criminal transgression of our laws (thus making it opposed to those laws) or of an accident (making it a random result or hiccup in an otherwise stable continuity). In either case the laws of the present are allowed to remain in place, with fascism something separate or even opposed to them. On the contrary, for Adorno, the 'true horror of fascism' is how close we are to it and how inseparable it can be from dominant Western ideology (insofar as such a thing exists). In this regard, the reading of fascist laughter given here is Adornaian since it refers similarly to laughter which reveals the fascist inherent to contemporary Western life.

In another way, Adorno's argument is not quite enough. As a result of the false distance between the world of the people laughing at Chaplin and the fascist world, Adorno argues that:

> *The Great Dictator* loses all satirical force, and becomes obscene, when a Jewish girl can bash a line of storm troopers on the head with a pan without being torn to pieces. For the sake of political commitment, political reality is trivialized: which then reduces the political effect.[5]

Thus, in a bizarre turn, these comedies themselves carry out what was discussed earlier in the book as a 'fascist joy' (the term of Jonathan Hall), rejecting and deriding the object of laughter, which is now, somewhat paradoxically, fascism itself. Adorno writes that in *Arturo Ui*, 'the ridicule to which Ui is consigned renders innocuous the fascism that was accurately predicted by Jack London decades before'.[6] To readers of Adorno, the tone of passage cannot help but recall the much more famous (and often misunderstood) comment made in 'Cultural Criticism and Society' that 'to write poetry after Auschwitz is barbaric'.[7] The statement was not – as it is often assumed to be – an attempt to silence poets and artists, just as these comments do not mean that we should end all comedy. Rather, they point to a fascist quality in all laughter, just as those more well-known comments pointed towards the fascism underneath the surface of a whole tradition of poetry. For Adorno and Horkheimer, writing in 'The Culture Industry', laughter, as a group activity, functions to produce a 'caricature of solidarity'.[8] Laughter is, at its very core, a fascist act. For Adorno, *all* laughter is fascist joy.

5 Ibid., p. 184.
6 Ibid.
7 Theodor Adorno, 'Cultural Criticism and Society', in *Prisms* (Cambridge, MA: MIT Press, 1983), pp. 17–34 (p. 34).
8 Theodor Adorno and Max Horkheimer, 'The Culture Industry: Enlightenment as Mass Deception', in *The Dialectics of Enlightenment*, ed. Gunzelin Schmid Noerr, trans. Edmund Jephcott (Stanford: Stanford University Press, 2002), pp. 94–136 (p. 112).

Adorno was not asking for a poetry which is not fascist, just as it would be difficult for us to ask for a laughter which had no fascist dimension. Rather, what Adorno asks us to do is to recognize the fascism within all laughter: a profoundly unfascist realization to make. Brecht and Chaplin, despite their radicalism, might not have recognized this. Certainly an entire history of theorists of laughter have failed to realize this, or have avoided doing so, perhaps to preserve laughter (or certain types of laughter) as something that is free, liberal and certainly not fascist. As discussed in detail earlier, the first of the three 'types' of laughter in 'type theory' is 'superiority theory' – the idea that we laugh in order to affirm our superiority over another. Such laughter is, first and foremost, cruel, and it may link laughter to fascism in a very broad way. The critical move of claiming this is only one 'type' of laughter allows theorists to invest positively in the idea of other laughter that is essentially liberating or radical and which avoids the limitations and dangers of other more 'reactionary' types of laughter such as those which are fascist. On the contrary, the powerful implication of Adorno's charge is that is it *this* laughter, any laughter which thinks it is separate from such ideologies, which is truly fascist.

Adorno's discussion is not without its own problems and inconsistencies. Despite the subtleties of his argument and the misunderstandings it has given rise to, Adorno *is* saying it would somehow be better if Brecht and Chaplin had not produced this kind of comedy, or at least that it might have been better if their comedy had been put together differently. Adorno's comments, no matter how insightful, may be guilty of believing in the possibility of a comedy that is free of such problematic distancing of the viewer from the target of the laughter, or in other words, a laughter which is not about sadistic cruelty even though he seems to be making the opposite claim. Indeed, his text uses the term 'wrong laughter', suggesting the possibility of a 'right laughter'. Alternatively, we can accept the anti-laughter reading of the argument, that all laughter should be avoided:

> In wrong society laughter is a sickness infecting happiness and drawing it into society's worthless totality. Laughter about something is always laughter at [sometimes translated as *deriding*] it, and the viral force which, according to Bergson, bursts through rigidity in laughter is, in truth, the irruption of barbarity, the self-assertion which, in convivial settings, dares to celebrate its liberation from scruple. The collective of those who laugh parodies humanity.[9]

[9] Ibid., p. 112.

And yet, if all laughter is dangerous fascist othering which makes us seem superior to what we laugh at, then why would Adorno direct a criticism to Brecht and Chaplin specifically, as if their particular type of 'wrong' comedy could have been otherwise? This book has discussed the dangers of 'type theory', and especially the idea that some laughter can be wrong and other laughter right. On the other hand, the idea of a society without laughter is unimaginable and the idea is itself funny (compare the Earl of Chesterfield's comments in Chapter 3). There may even be a slight hint of humour in Adorno's tirade against laughter.

So, what we are left with, it seems, it yet another divide between one laughter and another. On the one hand we have the idea (or possibility) of one laughter that *knows* it is fascist, a laughter which shows us how we are put together by imposing ideology in front of our eyes and making this visible to us (Benjamin's 'lining of the dress' in Chapter 2) and, on the other hand, a laughter which believes it is liberating, radical and anti-fascist, while having structural similarities to the very thing it claims to reject. This can also be considered in terms of laughter as event: there is laughter which knows it is an event, and laughter which pretends not to be. This is a vital point for this book and it has been my consistent claim throughout that seemingly radical laughter can have its own completely reactionary unconscious. With Adorno's help we can add that while the content of the comedy is often radical, liberating and even humane, its form and structure can be completely fascist.

This takes us back to the issues with which this book began. The introduction discussed the 'doubleness' in comedy, and perhaps we are now in a position to articulate the relationship in a more precise way to Milan Kundera, who wrote:

> Nowadays we don't realize that the same external display (that of laughter) serves two absolutely opposed internal attitudes. There are two laughters, and we have no word to tell one from the other.[10]

This book hopes to have provided a framework for discussing the different functions of laughter often held within the same laugh. In short, it suggests a new way of distinguishing between laughters: while certain kinds of laughter *know* themselves to be 'events' and make this visible to us, others *hide* their evental capacity. This distinction can be a useful way of assessing the political and social impacts of laughter. To put this in the context of a directly fascist joke (compare the discussion of racist jokes in Chapter 2), a joke always imposes and creates ideology (the ideology of 'us vs them', for example) but

[10] Kundera, *Book of Laughter*, p. 87.

it can either show us this creation of ideology (thus undermining it) or it can hide this evental creation of ideology from us (making it seem as if the laughter merely reflects a reality that is already there). As Athusser wrote, ideology never says 'I am Ideology'. Laughter sometimes does, while at other times it takes great care to hide the fact.

Despite the potential usefulness of this distinction, the idea of different kinds of laughter remains a dominant trend that I would like to resist. Perhaps unlike Adorno, I would certainly not prefer that Brecht or Chaplin's comedy was put together differently so that it belonged in a different category. On the contrary, it seems clear enough that one laughter can be both these things at once, or that one moment of laughter taken in both or either of these ways, depending on the context and individual experiencing the laughter in question. In other words, it is a difference of response rather than a difference in the joke or comedy itself. Alternatively we can say that while the joke or comedy remains the same, the laughter can change. Should Brecht and/or Chaplin have structured their comedy differently so that instead of causing a ridiculing and trivializing laughter *at* fascism which perhaps even affirms the viewer's own ideology over the fascist one that they target, their comedy would operate against the present, showing its viewers how fascist they themselves were? Would this be possible, what would it look like? Is laughing *at* fascism, to abject fascism, not acceptable in certain contexts, even if the laughter shares some structural similarity with the fascists themselves? To these difficult questions I would add a further one. Is it not the very laughter which thinks of itself as not fascist or as free of fascism which is in fact most fascist? How can the comedian or author ever ensure that audiences do not erupt into a fascist joy when laughing at the performance? In any case, my argument has been that laughter must always be both at once: that it must *be* an event and experienced as one (perhaps a fascist one) in order to *show* us an event (revealing the structure of our fascism).

There is nothing to prevent Chaplin's laughter, or our laughter at Chaplin's movie (fascist laughter according to Adorno) becoming properly anti-fascist, even without any changes to his films. In his 2006 film *The Pervert's Guide to Cinema*, Slavoj Žižek provides a reading of the film as a text that makes exactly the point that Adorno seems to want it to make. Žižek argues for the films comic radicalism, and ultimately sees it as a critique not only of fascism but of the forms of humanity and democracy that are usually thought of as so opposed to fascism. At the end of the movie, Chaplin, who plays two characters in the film (a Jewish barber and Hitler) is on stage in his barber character at a Nazi rally, but the audience all believe that he is Hitler. He delivers his speech in the name of democracy:

> I'm sorry, but I don't want to be an emperor.
> That's not my business.
> I don't want to rule or conquer anyone.
> I should like to help everyone, if possible.
> Jew, gentile, black man, white, we all want to help one another.
> Human beings are like that...
> Soldiers, in the name of democracy, let us all unite![11]

Žižek makes the important point that 'people applaud exactly in the same way as they were applauding Hitler'. He goes on to discuss the role of music in the film, noting that:

> The music that accompanies this great humanist finale, the overture to Wagner's opera, Lohengrin, is the same music as the one we hear when Hitler is daydreaming about conquering the entire world and where he has a balloon in the shape of the globe.[12]

Žižek's point here is that the celebration of democracy, fraternity and human equality can be *felt* in much the same way as the celebration of fascism, Nazism and the violent expulsion of the other. For Žižek, Chaplin's film works to show us this, rather than hide it from us (making the interpretation completely opposed to that of Adorno). In making us *feel* for democracy in the same way as others *feel* for fascism, the close structural link between the two ostensibly opposite political systems is revealed. Žižek explains:

> This can be read as the ultimate redemption of music, that the same music which served evil purposes can be redeemed to serve the good. Or it can be read, and I think it should be read, in a much more ambiguous way, that with music, we cannot ever be sure. In so far as it externalizes our inner passion, music is potentially always a threat.[13]

What this shows is that we experience rallying speeches and music in structurally similar ways, even when the content is completely changed. In this case Chaplin changes the content of the speech into the absolute opposite of what the Nazis expect it to be, delivering from Hilter's mouth a speech about equality and democracy. Despite the radical change in content, the

[11] *The Great Dictator*, dir. Charlie Chaplin (USA: United Artists, 1940), 1 hour 59 minutes.
[12] *The Pervert's Guide to Cinema*, dir. Sophie Fiennes (UK: Mischief Films, 2006). 20 minutes.
[13] Ibid., 21 minutes.

response of the audience is the same. This would have obviously significance for jokes, where the content is often changed while the form remains the same. Chapter 2 discussed how jokes English people tell about Scottish people are told in Scotland about people from Aberdeen, while Adorno's point is that jokes about a fascist may not be the opposite to jokes about a Jew. And yet, the rereading of the humour in *The Great Dictator* makes it into exactly what Adorno felt it was not: not a celebration of American humanity as the opposite of fascism but a warning that the two might be closer than we often think.

Žižek's observations about the way we are stimulated into affectual passion by the emotional movements of music may very much comparably describe the process of laughter. However, I am not arguing Žižek's corner in the Adorno disagreement. The final argument of the book aims to show how Žižek's reading eventally operates on the laughter he interprets, changing it. As such, it is not that Žižek is right about Chaplin and indeed Adorno's reading is probably more politically important. However, the examples of Adorno and Žižek's diametrically opposed experiences of the laughter created by Chaplin's movie show a limitation of existing discussions of laughter. The two opposed readings, both valid, undermine the idea of laughter as inherently *this* or *that*: liberation or control. Instead, they show that laughter can be several things at once. The question is whether we are aware of both the directions in which laughter pulls, to laughter's dialectical quality, its ability to be ideological and yet at the same time make the hidden structures of ideology visible to us.

If every laugh is different, it becomes impossible to criticize a comedian for the type or effect of laughter that they stimulate in their readers/audiences/viewers. In this regard the reader might by now be convinced by the claim made in the introduction of this book: that it can be the shared connections between our laughs that are most important, rather than the differences between each laugh. Adorno can usefully reflect on the laughter that Brecht might have tended to stimulate, even if each of the concrete individuals laughing at his plays differently. And yet, at the same time, arguments about what Chaplin's comedy was *really* like, whether it was radical, left wing or fascist, risk separating the laughter from its interpretations, as if the laughter itself carries within in a quality, be that a quality of fascism, liberation, humanity or indeed anything else.

What we see instead is that laughter is never separable from its interpretations. Perhaps this is why interpretations of laughter can be so compelling and how those writing on laughter can so often seem to hit the nail on the head, as if their interpretation strikes at the heart of what the example of laughter in question is really about and shows all prior explanations to be problematic. In this book I have interpreted many jokes and moments of comedy, and even more have been tested on friends and colleagues. It has always struck me as unsettling how utterly convinced people are by each interpretation of laughter I attempted, even when I have known these interpretations to be very insecure and provisional. This points not so much to laughter's infinite unknowability or multiplicity, as Bataille might have argued, but rather to the 'evental' relationship between laughter and its interpretations. If laughter is interpreted in such and such a way, it begins to function in exactly that way, also seeming, as I have argued above, to have always already had that function. Like Bernhard's narrator who could never think of Einstein without his tongue out after seeing that famous image, once a joke has been convincingly explained, that joke can never been seen without the explanation attached.

Even more than this, previous interpretations of laughter, as well as general ideas surrounding its functions, assumptions about its roles and its causes and effects, all play a role in its actual effect on us and the way we experience it. Interpretations of laughter do far more than decode and reveal what is already happening when we laugh. Indeed, they eventally and retroactively transform laughter into something that from then on it always already appears to have been. Yet, we are not free to say whatever we like about laughter, and interpretations can certainly be 'wrong'. This is because the conscious and unconscious assumptions about laughter's functions held by any given time or place into which laughter erupts govern and influence the way in which that laughter is experienced. In other words, it is not only our isolated interpretation of laughter that matters but the other interpretations and assumptions about laughter, both conscious and unconscious, which determine the effects of each laugh. Our 'interpretations' of laughter, what we think it does, whether we are consciously aware of these interpretations or not, effect how we experience laughter and how it affects us. On this note however, laughter is different to literature when it comes to the role of the author. Literary studies have long recognized Roland Barthes's effacement of the author, but Foucault's concept of an 'author function' is still vital as a reminder that one cannot interpret a text freely and individually. The laugh moves much more authorlessly through time and space, even if we still attach comedy to its owners.

Seeing laughter as event is not just another compelling interpretation, which refutes others and asserts its own validity, finally ending discussions of what laughter is really about. On the contrary, to say that laughter should be thought of in terms of the event is the beginning of the discussion rather than the end. As I hope to have shown over the course of this book, it is vital to recognize the evental capacity of laughter for many reasons. Broadly speaking, these reasons can put these into three main camps.

First, ideas of laughter as essentially having this or that quality within it, whether that quality be liberating, controlling, fascist or democratizing, often misses the complex effects that laughter has. These ideas almost always see laughter as a response to *existing* conditions, whether this laughter-as-response is a liberating rejection of these conditions or an ideological assertion of them. Seeing laughter as an event allows us to explore the fact that laughter is clearly not only an effect but also an event that has the power to retroactively change the world it interrupts, sometimes even changing its own causes.

Second, the tendency to hide or ignore laughter's evental power has served what I would consider to be largely reactionary and ideologically dangerous agendas. This book has shown that laughter can bring things into being *eventally*, creating hierarchies, identities, relationships and subject-positions. This movement in itself can be neither good nor evil, or it can be good or evil depending on the interpretations of any number of interested parties. My point is that because laughter brings things into being it can be a point at which those things can be seen coming into being, making laughter full of anxiety and insecurity because it shows how fragile these things can be and how easily things can be taken down and recreated. On the other hand, ignoring or failing to see the evental power of laughter has served the opposite purpose. Laughter has been seen as evidence of how things are, it has been a force that secures individuals and a force that naturalizes relationships between people and things, making them seem inevitable and irrefutable.

Third, laughter can have many functions and effects, often diverse and sometimes simultaneous. Just as importantly, these effects of laughter are subject to evental change. The implications of this third observation are particularly important for those studying comedy or those discussing it, as interpretations of laughter need to recognize their role in influencing the effects of laughter. However, this does not apply only to academics and theorists in the field of 'laughter studies', which I hope will be a growing field, but to interpretations of laughter in a much broader sense. Culturally circulating ideas about laughter effect the experience of laughter in that culture, and these ideas are created not only by theorists and critics of laughter but by general discussion from comedians to fridge magnets. Cultural clichés pinned to our fridges proclaiming phrases such as 'Live. Laugh. Love' will affect how laughter will be experienced in such a culture, associating it with positivity and emotionality and framing it as a 'genuine' experience. The idea that it is 'beautiful' to see children laughing is another such cliché that embodies the assumptions we make about laughter but also reinforces them: we are forced by such innocent utterances to see laughter as natural, the province of children, and as something positive and celebratory. Seeing laughter as an event means insisting that we become aware of this relationship between laughter and what it said about it.

A history of laughter

This final point, that laughter is transformed by readings of laughter, raises another issue for studies of laughter: the idea of a history of laughter. The evental relationship between laughter and its interpretations is an important one, and one that helps to unpack the problem of a history of laughter. Can laughter be historicized? Can we discuss the changes in laughter that might have occurred over time, how laughter's role or roles have developed or changed in the course of history? Can we speak of any continuity when it comes to something as discontinuous as laughter?

The issue of whether one could write a history of laughter is a question raised by the quotation given as an epigraph above, originally from the influential Russian critic Alexander Herzen but more famously quoted by Bakhtin. The question of a history of laughter foregrounds the problem that is easy to regard laughter as apolitical and outside of history, as if it is natural, as both ancient and recent writers have tended to do. This problem has a whole history behind it and has characterized many discussions of laughter; even Hegel has seen comedy as outside of the dialectic (which in Hegel's terms is almost synonymous with the political). Much recent work on laughter has maintained that there is a certain consistency in laughter across history, even claiming that there may not be a 'history of laughter' because laughter is a trait of 'human nature', which can be seen as unchanging.[14] This reduces the radicalism of laughter by making it appear to be something natural and constant, and it also ignores the possible dangers of highly political laughter. At best this way of seeing laughter encourages us to ignore its political dimensions, while at worst it establishes a dangerous conception of 'human nature' often based on the cruel rejection of others, as shown throughout this book. If laughter is seen as natural, then it takes on the dangerous ability to naturalize ideologically questionable and cruel structures that laughter seems to reflect.

[14] See the introduction in Manfred Pfister (ed.), *A History of English Laughter: Laughter from Beowulf to Beckett and Beyond* (New York and Amsterdam: Rodopi, 2002), p. v.

Laughter has effects that correspond to the feelings ideas about its effects held by the society, moment and culture into which that laughter erupts. To abbreviate this point, we can say that a society in which laughter is seen as positive and liberating may experience laughter in that way because of those beliefs about laughter. Likewise, a society which sees laughter as a natural reaction to ugliness will experience laughter as confirmation that the target of laughter is ugly and inferior. On a more complex level, any given social structure will hold a number of contradictory assumptions about laughter, many of which are entirely unconscious, which will affect how individual events of laughter operate in that specific and particular context.

Thus, a history of laughter, or any attempt to study the laughter of a moment other than our own, must be attentive to at least three often contradictory things. First, it must try to be attentive to the beliefs about laughter held by the moment into the moments of laughter erupt. This can be a difficult and even impossible thing to discover, since many of our assumptions about laughter are unconscious but nevertheless influence laughter's effects. Second, such studies must be attentive to the assumptions made about laughter in our own moment and how those are forced onto the laughter we discuss, eventally transforming it. This can again be near impossible, given that we are often unaware of our own unconscious assumptions about laughter. Third, in the case of literature at least, there is the question of the author's judgment in the original text and the expected judgement of the original reader. Seventeenth-century readers of Don Quixote, for example, might have been okay with laughter's cruelty (at Sancho Panza's physical pain, for example) but the nineteenth-century reader may not have been, unless they are like Thackeray, who seemed to like the idea that laughter was a way of combatting the inferior: 'some there are, and very successful too, mere quacks and fools: and it was to combat and expose such as those no doubt that Laughter was made'.[15] However, as I have shown, what the author thinks their laugher does and how they imagine the reader will consume it is only part of the event of laughter. Since laughter divorces itself from its author and from those who originally laughed, such arguments about literature miss the ability of laughter to escape its context in a way that literature perhaps cannot.

The answer to questions such as 'is laughter in Shakespeare radical?' has nothing to do with identifying the true characteristics inherent to Shakespeare's comedy or whether his work is essentially or ultimately radical or not. Žižek can quite easily turn a given joke from the text into a radical

[15] William Makepeace Thackeray, *Vanity Fair*, ed. John Sutherland (Oxford: Oxford World's Classics, 1983), p. 96.

anti-capitalist gesture, while Adorno might be able to prove that the same joke is completely capitalist. Two people might be able to laugh at the joke in completely different ways, proving both interpretations to be valid. We could say that just as laughter interpellates us, we interpellate laughter. Studies of comedy have tended to endlessly fall into the question of whether laughter is radical or conservative, with both sides of the discussion making valid arguments. This plays itself out in discussions of single authors. The subject of my PhD was Charles Dickens, and some Dickens critics are so divided as to whether Dickens's humour is radical or reactionary that they fall out with each other at academic conferences when discussing the subject. What we need in order to begin discussing such questions, questions of a history of laughter, is a double analysis of the ways in which laughter eventally transformed things within its moment and the ways in which that laughter is now eventally transformed again by new interpretations that we impose upon it.

The relationship between interpreting laughter and the laughter that is under interpretation can be seen as what Walter Benjamin calls a 'constellation', itself a kind of event that makes it apparent to us that past and present, like laughter and the meanings we attach to it, are always in a dialectical rather than linear relationship. Benjamin's idea of a constellation is designed to provide an alternative way of discussing the relationship between the present and history, and it is a vital tool when it comes to the history of laughter. In laughter at the past or at something considered 'old', two moments connect and illuminate each other, producing a new relationship and changing both past and present in the moment of connection, a Benjamininan 'constellation'. The term is used in Benjamin's work to refer to the relationship which emerges when the historian places two apparently unrelated historical events in a significant connection with each other.[16] At this moment a 'constellation' emerges, which Benjamin describes as a flash of recognition that involves a leap in historical understanding, which sheds light on the meaning of both periods, also changing both. It we are to have a 'history of laughter' then, it cannot be linear but must be constellational, since the present influences the past as much as the past influences the present, with meaning constructed anew in the flash of this connection. Laughter itself is a flash of constellational recognition which transforms the relationship between the then and the now.

Seeing laughter as an event, as I hope to have shown to be necessary, involves recognising this transformative function that laughter has in its relationship to history and to the past. To push the point to an extreme,

[16] Benjamin, *The Arcades Project*, p. 462.

I argue that every laugh is a miniature version of what Michel Foucault calls an 'epistemic shift', a moment at which history itself is changed and access to the past as it previously was becomes impossible. The concept of the event has been used to describe a moment which changes the world around it, breaking the existing relationship between past and present and reconstituting both in a new constellation. Laughter is exactly such an event.

There are many kinds of event, probably more than Badiou knew of, many things which burst into the present and reorder and restructure our world as we know it, making it impossible to see things as they previously were. Not all of these events are funny and most are very far from being so. Instead, events tend to be shocking and violent, destructive and dangerous, even traumatic. Laughter then, is not just one of many such events. On the contrary, laughter is a unique and important kind of event, one that operates on us carefully and unconsciously, often appearing innocent, harmless and light while it subtly and powerfully configures how we see ourselves and who we are. Unlike many events, laughter often hides from us the dangerous fact that we experience it as an event, appearing to us as small and inconsequential. Unaware of its significance and power, laughter can get us from anywhere and we have little or no agency in the matter. On the other hand, laughter can make us see events for what they are, making visible yet another shift in our transient and incrementally reconfigured identities. What should we do in the event of laughter? If I have shown just one thing in this book I hope it is this: we should never let the event of laughter go lightly, because it may be one of the most powerful events of all.

Bibliography

Adorno, Theodor, *Aesthetic Theory*, trans. Robert Hullot-Kentor (Minneapolis: University of Minnesota Press, 1997).

Adorno, Theodor, 'Commitment', in *Aesthetics and Politics*, ed. Theodor Adorno et al. (London: Verso, 2007), pp. 177–96.

Adorno, Theodor, 'Cultural Criticism and Society', in *Prisms* (Cambridge, MA: MIT Press, 1983), pp. 17–34.

Adorno, Theodor, *Notes to Literature*, ed. Rolf Tiedemann (New York: Columbia University Press, 1974).

Adorno, Theodor, and Max Horkheimer, 'The Culture Industy: Enlightenment as Mass Deception', in *The Dialectics of Enlightenment*, ed. Gunzelin Schmid Noerr, trans. Edmund Jephcott (Stanford: Stanford Univeristy Press, 2002), pp. 94–136.

Alfred, David, 'The Comedy of Innocence', in *The Strumpet Muse: Art and Morals in Chaucer's Poetry* (Bloomington: Indiana University Press, 1976), pp. 90–107.

Althusser, Louis, *The Future Lasts a Long Time*, ed. Olivier Corpet and Yann Moulier Boutang, trans. Richard Veasey (London: Vintage, 1994).

Althusser, Louis, *Lenin and Philosophy and Other Essays*, trans. Ben Brewster (New York: Monthly Review Press, 2001).

Althusser, Louis, *The Spectre of Hegel: Early Writings*, ed. Francois Matheron, trans. G. M. Goshgarian (London: Verso, 2014).

Andreas, J. R., 'The Rhetoric of Chaucerian Comedy: The Aristotelian Legacy', *Comparatist*, vol. 8 (1984), pp. 56–66.

Andrews, Malcolm, *Dickensian Laughter: Essays on Dickens and Humour* (Oxford: Oxford University Press, 2013).

Aristophanes, *Lysistrata and Other Plays*, ed. and trans. Alan H. Sommerstein (London: Penguin, 2002).

Aristotle, *The Basic Works of Aristotle*, ed. Richard McKeon (New York: Random House, 1941).

Aristotle, *On the Parts of Animals I–IV*, trans. James G. Lennox (Oxford: Oxford University Press, 2001).

Aristotle, 'Poetics', in *The Norton Anthology of Theory and Criticism*, ed. Vincent B. Leitch (London: W. W. Norton, 2001), pp. 88–115.

Badiou, Alain, *Being and Event*, trans. Oliver Feltham (London: Continuum, 2005).

Bailey, Peter, *Leisure and Class in Victorian England: Rational Recreation and the Contest for Control, 1830–1885* (New York: Routledge, 2007).

Bakhtin, Mikhail, 'Characteristics of Plot Composition in Dostoevsky's Works', in *Fyodor Dostoevsky's Crime and Punishment*, ed. Harold Bloom (New York: Infobase Publishing, 2004), pp. 33–87.

Bakhtin, Mikhail, *Rabelais and His World*, trans. Helene Iswolsky (Bloomington, IN: Indiana University Press, 1984).

Baudelaire, Charles, *The Painter of Modern Life and Other Essays* (London: Phaidon Press, 2006).

Benjamin, Andrew, *The Plural Event: Descartes, Hegel, Heidegger* (London: Routledge, 2005).

Benjamin, Walter, *The Arcades Project*, trans. Rolf Tiedemann (Cambridge, MA: Harvard University Press, 1999).

Benjamin, Walter, *The Origin of German Tragic Drama*, trans. John Osbourne (London and New York: Verso, 2009).

Benjamin, Walter, *Selected Writings Volume One: 1913–1926*, ed. Marcus Bullock and Michael W. Jennings (Cambridge, MA: Harvard University Press, 2014).

Bergson, Henri, *Laughter: An Essay on the Meaning of the Comic*, trans. Cloudesely Brereton and Fred Rothwell (Rockville: Arc Manor, 2008).

Billig, Michael, 'Comic Racism and Violence', in *Beyond a Joke: The Limits of Humour*, ed. Sharon Lockyer and Michael Pickering (New York: Palgrave Macmillan, 2005), pp. 25–44.

Billig, Michael, 'Humour and Hatred: The Racist Jokes of the Ku Klux Klan', *Discourse and Society*, vol. 12 (2001), pp. 267–89.

Billig, Michael, *Laughter and Ridicule: Towards a Social Critique of Humour* (London: Sage, 2005).

Billington, J. H., *The Icon and the Axe: An Interpretive History of Russian Culture* (New York: Vintage Books, 1970).

Borch-Jacobsen, Mikkel, 'The Laughter of Being', in *Bataille: A Critical Reader*, ed. Fred Botting and Scott Wilson (Oxford: Blackwell, 1991), pp. 146–66.

Brecht, Bertolt, *Gessamelte Werke*, vol. 14 (Frankfurt: Suhrkamp, 1967).

Brennecke, Ernest, *Shakespeare in Germany 1500–1700, with Translations of Five Early Plays* (Chicago: University of Chicago Press, 1964).

Buchan, Suzanne, 'Theatrical Cartoon Comedy: From Animated Potmantaeu to the *Risis Purus*', in *A Companion to Film Comedy*, ed. Andrew Horton and Joanna E. Rapf (Oxford: Wiley Blackwell, 2012), pp. 521–44.

Buck-Morss, Susan, *The Dialectics of Seeing: Walter Benjamin and the Arcades Project* (Cambridge, MA: MIT Press, 1989).

Butler, Judith, *Gender Trouble* (London: Routledge, 1990).

Carlyle, Thomas, *Sartor Resartus*, ed. Kerry McSweeney and Peter Sabor (Oxford: Oxford University Press, 1999).

Carroll, Noël, *Comedy Incarnate: Buster Keaton, Physical Comedy and Bodily Coping* (Oxford: Blackwell, 2007).

Carroll, Noël, *A Very Short Introduction to Humour* (Oxford: Oxford University Press, 2014).

Chaplin, Charlie (dir.), *The Great Dictator* (USA: United Artists, 1940).

Chiaro, Delia, *The Language of Jokes: Analysing Verbal Play* (London: Routledge, 1992).

Collier, John Payne, *Punch and Judy: A Short History with the Original Dialogue* (Nineola, NY: Dover, 2006).

Coogan, Tom, and Rebecca Mallett (eds), 'Disability, Humour and Comedy,' *Journal of Literary & Cultural Disability Studies*, vol. 7, no. 3 (2013).

Cooper, Anthony Ashley, Earl of Shaftesbury, *Characteristicks of Men, Manners, Opinions, Times*, ed. Douglas den Uyl (Indianapolis: Liberty Fund, 2001).

Critchley, Simon, 'Comedy and Finitute', in *Ethics, Politics, Subjectivity: Essays on Derrida, Levinas and Contemporary French Thought* (London: Verso, 1999), pp. 217–38.

Critchley, Simon, *On Humour* (London: Routledge, 2002).

Crone, Rosalind, 'Mr and Mrs Punch in Nineteenth-Century England', *Historical Journal*, vol. 49, no. 4 (2006), pp. 1055–82.

Davis, Murray S., *What's So Funny? The Comic Conception of Culture and Society* (Chicago: Chicago University Press, 1993).

Deleyto, Celestino, 'Humor and Erotic Utopia: The Intimate Scenarios of Romantic Comedy', in *A Companion to Film Comedy*, ed. Andrew Horton and Joanna E. Rapf (Oxford: Wiley Blackwell, 2012), pp. 175–95.

Derrida, Jacques, *Glas*, trans. R. Rand (Nebraska: University of Nebraska Press, 1986).

Derrida, Jacques, *The Postcard: From Socrates to Freud and Beyond* (London: University of Chicago Press, 1987).

Derrida, Jacques, ' "To Do Justice to Freud": The History of Madness in the Age of Psychoanalysis', in *Resistances of Psychoanalysis*, trans Peggy Kamuf, Pascale-Anne Brault and Michael Nass (California: Stanford University Press, 1998), pp. 70–118.

Derrida, Jacques, *Writing and Difference*, trans. Alan Bass (London: Routledge, 2001).

Dickens, Charles, *Barnaby Rudge*, ed. John Bowen (London: Penguin, 2003).

Dickens, Charles, *Little Dorrit*, ed. Helen Small (London: Penguin, 2003).

Dickens, Charles, *The Old Curiosity Shop*, ed. Norman Page (London: Penguin, 2000).

Dickie, Simon, *Cruelty and Laughter: Forgotten Comic Literature and the Unsentimental Eighteenth-Century* (Chicago: University of Chicago Press, 2011).

Dodds, E. R., *The Greeks and the Irrational* (London: University of California Press, 1951).

Dolar, Mladen, 'Comedy and Its Double', in *Schluss mit der Komodie! Zue sch,leichenden Vorherrschaft des Tragischen in unserer Kultur (Stop That Comedy! On the Subtle Hegemony of the Tragic in Our Culture)*, ed. Robert Pfaller (Wien: Slonderzahl, 2005), pp. 181–210.

Dolar, Mladen, 'The Owl of Minerva from Dusk till Dawn, or, Two Shades of Gray', *Filozofija i društvo*, vol. 26, no. 4 (2015), pp. 875–90.

Dolar, Mladen, 'Strel sredi koncerta' in Theodor Adorno, *Uvod v sociologijo glasbe* (Ljubljana: DZS, 1986), pp. 301–64.

Donaldson, Ian, *The World Upside-Down: Comedy from Jonson to Fielding* (Oxford: Oxford University Press, 1970).
Eagleton, Terry, *Water Benjamin, or Towards a Revolutionary Criticism* (London: Verso, 1981).
Eco, Umberto, 'The Frames of Comic "Freedom"', in *Carnival!*, ed. Thomas A. Seboek (Berlin: Mouton, 1984), pp. 1–9.
English, James, *Comic Transactions: Literature, Humour and the Politics of Community in Twentieth-Century Britain* (Ithaca: Cornell University Press, 1994).
Evans, Dylan, *An Introductory Dictionary of Lacanian Terms* (London: Routledge, 1996).
Farrell, Thomas J. (ed.), *Bakhtin and Medieval Voices* (Florida: University of Florida Press, 1995).
Fiennes, Sophie (dir.), *The Pervert's Guide to Cinema* (UK: Mischief Films, 2006).
Foucault, Michel, *Discipline and Punish: The Birth of the Prison*, trans. Alan Sheridan (London: Penguin, 1977).
Foucault, Michel, *The History of Madness*, ed. Jean Khalfa, trans. Jonathan Murphy and Jean Khalfa (Oxon: Routledge, 2006).
Foucault, Michel, 'My Body, This Paper, This Fire', trans. Geoff Bennington in *Oxford Literary Review*, vol. 4, no. 1 (August 1971), pp. 9–28.
Foucault, Michel, *The Order of Things* (London: Routledge, 2002).
Freud, Sigmund, *The Standard Edition of the Complete Psychological Works of Sigmund Freud*, ed. and trans. James Strachey et al., 24 vols (London: Vintage, 2001).
Frye, Northrop, *Anatomy of Criticism* (Princeton: Princeton University Press, 1957).
Fung, Paul, *Dostoevsky and the Epileptic Mode of Being* (London: Legenda, 2015).
Gearhart, Suzanne, 'The Remnants of Philosophy: Psychoanalysis after *Glas*', in *Hegel after Derrida*, ed. Stuart Barnett (London: Routledge, 1998), pp. 147–70.
Gilhus, Ingvild, *Laughing Gods, Weeping Virgins: Laughter in the History of Religion* (London: Routledge, 1997).
Girard, Rene, 'A Perilous Balance: A Comic Hypothesis', Comparative Literature, *MLN*, vol. 87, no. 7 (December 1972), pp. 811–26.
Goethe, Johann Wolfgang von, *Elective Affinities* (New York: Henry Holt, 1872).
Goffman, Erving, *Frame Analysis* (New York: Harper, 1974).
Gogol, Nikolai, *The Collected Tales of Nikolai Gogol* (Vintage: New York, 1999), pp. 394–424.
Gruner, Charles, *The Game of Humour: A Comprehensive Theory of Why We Laugh* (London: Transaction, 2000).
Gruner, Charles, *Understanding Laughter: The Workings of Wit and Humour* (Chicago: Nelson-Hall, 1978).

Gryphius, Andreas, *Carolus Stuardus*, ed. Hugh Powell (Leicester: University College Leicester Press, 1955).
Haddon, Mark, *The Curious Incident of the Dog in the Night-Time* (London: Vintage, 2003).
Hall, Jonathan, *Anxious Pleasures* (London: Associated University Press, 1995).
Halliwell, Stephen, 'The Uses of Laughter in Greek Culture', *Classical Quarterly*, vol. 41, no. 2 (1991), pp. 279–96.
Hallward, Peter, *Badiou: A Subject to Truth* (London: University of Minnesota Press, 2003).
Hazlitt, William, *Lectures on the English Comic Writers* (London: Taylor and Hessey, 1819).
Hegel, G. W. F., *Aesthetics, vol. II*, trans T. M. Knox (Oxford: Clarendon Press, 1975).
Hegel, G. W. F., *Hegel: The Letters*, trans. Clark Butler and Christiane Seiler (Bloomington: Indiana University Press, 1984).
Hegel, G. W. F., *Hegel's Phenomenology of Spirit*, trans. A. V. Miller (Oxford: Oxford University Press, 1977).
Hegel, G. W. F., *The Logic of Science*, trans. George di Giovanni (Cambridge: Cambridge University Press, 2010).
Heine, Heinrich, 'Briefe über Deutschland', in *Sämtliche Schriften*, vol. 5 (Munich: Hanser, 1976), pp. 199–205.
Heller, Agnes, *Immortal Comedy: The Comic Phenomenon in Art, Literature and Life* (Oxford: Lexington Books, 2005).
Henkle, Roger B., *Comedy and Culture: England 1820–1900* (Princeton: Princeton University Press, 1980).
Hobbes, Thomas, *Leviathan* (Indiana: Hackett, 1994).
Hokensen, Jan, *The Idea of Comedy: History, Theory, Comedy* (Madison: Fairleigh Dickinson University Press, 2006).
Hölderlin, Friedrich, *Essays and Letters on Theory*, ed. and trans. Thomas Pfau (Albany: SUNY Press, 1988).
Howitt, Dennis, and Kwame Owusu-Bempah, 'Race and Ethnicity in Popular Humour', in *Beyond a Joke: The Limits of Humour*, ed. Sharon Lockyer and Michael Pickering (New York: Palgrave Macmillan, 2005), pp. 45–62.
Kafka, Franz, *Letters to Felice*, ed. Erich Heller and Jurgen Born, trans. James Stern and Elizabeth Duckworth (New York: Schocken Boks, 1973).
Kafka, Franz, *The Trial*, trans. Idris Parry (London: Penguin, 2000).
Kazantzakis, Nikos, *Zorba the Greek* (New York: Simon and Schuster, 1952).
Kierkegaard, Soren, *The Concept of Anxiety*, ed. and trans. Reidar Thomte (Princeton: Princeton University Press, 1980).
Kojeve, Alexandre, *Introduction to the Reading of Hegel*, ed. Allan Bloom, trans. James H. Nichols, Jr (New York: Basic Books, 1969).
Konzett, Matthias (ed.), *Encyclopedia of German Literature* (Chicago: Fitzroy Dearborn, 2000).
Kowsar, Mohammad, 'Lacan and Claudel: Desire and "The Hostage"', *Theatre Journal*, vol. 46, no. 1 (March 1994), pp. 79–93.

Kris, Ernst, *Psychoanalytic Explorations in Art* (London: George Allen & Unwin, 1953).
Kristeva, Julia, *Powers of Horror: An Essay on Abjection*, trans. Leon S. Roudiez (New York: Columbia University Press, 1982).
Kristeva, Julia, *Revolution in Poetic Language*, trans. Margaret Waller (New York: Columbia University Press, 1984).
Kundera, Milan, *The Book of Laughter and Forgetting*, trans. Alan Asher (London: Faber and Faber, 1996).
Lacan, Jacques, *Anxiety*, ed. Jacques Alain-Miller (Cambridge: Polity Press, 2014).
Lacan, Jacques, *Ecrits: A Selection*, trans. Alan Sheridan, (London: Routledge, 1989).
Lacan, Jacques, *The Ethics of Psychoanalysis*, ed. Jacques Alain-Miller, trans. Dennis Porter (London: Norton, 1992).
Lacan, Jacques, *The Four Fundamental Concepts of Psychoanalysis*, ed. Jacques Alain-Miller, trans. Alan Sheridan (London: Norton, 1998).
Lacan, Jacques, *The Other Side of Psychoanalysis*, ed. Jacques Alain-Miller, trans. Russel Grigg (London: Norton, 2007).
Lacan, Jacques, 'The Tokyo Discourse', *Journal for Lacanian Studies*, vol. 3, no. 1, (2005), pp. 129–44.
Lacoue-Labarthe, Phillipe, 'The Caesura of the Speculative', in *Typography: Mimesis, Philosophy, Politics*, ed. Christopher Fynsk (Massachusets: Harvard University Press, 1989), pp. 208–35.
Laroque, Francois, *Shakespeare's Festive World* (Cambridge: Cambridge University Press, 2003).
Le Gof, Jacques, 'Laughter in the Middle Ages', in *A Cultural History of Humour*, ed. Jan Bremmer and Herman Roodenburg (Oxford: Polity, 1997), pp. 40–53.
Leconte, Daniel, and Emmanuel Leconte (dir.), *Je Suis Charlie* (France: Films en Stock, 2015).
Lefcourt, H. M., and R. A. Martin, *Humor and Life Stress: Antidote to Adversity* (New York: Springer-Verlag, 1986).
Lehman, K. M., K. L. Burke, R. Martin, J. Sultan and D. R. Czech, 'A Reformulation of the Moderating Effects of Productive Humor', *Humor: International Journal of Humor Research*, vol. 14 (2001), pp. 131–61.
Lipovetsky, Gilles, *The Empire of Fashion: Dressing Modern Democracy*, trans. Catherine Porter (Princeton: Princeton University Press, 1994).
Lipps, Theodor, *Komik und Humor: Eine psychologisch-asthetische* (Hamburg und Leipzig: L. Voss, 2005).
Mannoni, Octave, 'I Know Well, but All the Same…', trans. G. M. Goshgarian, in *Perversion and the Social Relation*, ed. Molly Anne Rothenberg, Dennis A. Foster and Slavoj Žižek (Durham: Duke University Press, 2003), pp. 68–92.
Martin, R. A., *The Psychology of Humor: An Integrative Approach* (Burlington, MA: Elsevier Academic Press, 2007).

Mauron, Charles, *Psychocritque du Genre Comique* (Paris: Libraire Jose Corti, 1964).
McGowan, Todd, *The Feminine 'No!': Psychoanalysis and the New Canon* (Albany: SUNY Press, 2001).
Medhurst, Andy, *A National Joke: Popular Comedy and English Cultural Identities* (London: Routledge, 2007).
Milner, Jean-Claude, *L'Œuvre claire: Lacan, la science, la philosophie* (Paris: Éditions du Seuil, 1995).
Morreall, John, *Comedy, Tragedy and Religion* (Albany: SUNY Press, 1999).
Morreall, John, *Taking Laughter Seriously* (Albany: SUNY Press, 1983).
Moussaieff Masson, Jeffrey (ed.), *The Complete Letters of Sigmund Freud to Wilhelm Fleiss* (Cambridge, MA: Belknap Press, 1986).
Nancy, Jean-Luc, 'Elliptical Sense', *Research in Phenomenology*, vol. 18 (1988), pp. 175–91.
Nancy, Jean-Luc, 'Wild Laughter in the Throat of Death', *MLN*, vol. 103, no. 4 (September 1987), pp. 719–36.
North, Michael, *Machine-Age Comedy* (Oxford: Oxford University Press, 2009).
Norwood, Gilbert, *Greek Comedy* (London: Methuen, 1931).
Olson, Elder, *The Theory of Comedy* (Bloomington: Indiana University Press, 1968).
Palmer, D. J. (ed.), *Comedy: Developments in Criticism* (London: Macmillan, 1984).
Parker, Ian, and David Pavon-Cuellar, *Lacan, Discourse, Event: New Psychoanalytic Approaches to Textual Indeterminacy* (London: Routledge, 2013).
Parker, Ian, and David Pavon-Cuellar, 'Lacanian Domains of Practice and Forms of Event in Analysis', in *Lacan, Discourse, Event*, ed. Ian Parker and David Pavon-Cuéllar (London: Routledge, 2013), pp. 338–46.
Parvulescu, Anca, *Laughter: Notes on a Passion* (Cambridge, MA: MIT Press, 2010).
Parvulescu, Anca, 'Kafka's Laughter: On Joy and the Kafkaesque', *PMLA*, vol. 130, no. 5 (October 2015), pp. 1420–32.
Patten, Robert L., *George Cruikshanks Life, Times and Art, vol 1* (London: Lutterworth Press, 1992).
Paul, Jean, *Jean Paul: A Reader*, ed. Timothy J. Casey, trans. Erika Casey (London: Johns Hopkins University Press, 1992).
Pepys, Samuel, *The Diary of Samuel Pepys*, ed. Richard Le Gallienne (New York: Modern Library, 2003).
Pfister, Manfred (ed.), *A History of English Laughter: Laughter from Beowulf to Beckett and Beyond* (New York and Amsterdam: Rodopi, 2002).
Potter, Stephen, *The Sense of Humour* (London: Penguin Books, 1954).
Rickels, Laurence, *Abberations of Mourning* (London: University of Minnesota Press, 2011).
Rose, Gillian, *Hegel Contra Sociology* (London: Verso, 2009).

Salingar, Leo, *Shakespeare and the Tradition of Comedy* (Cambridge: Cambridge University Press, 1974).
Salisbury, Laura, '"SO THE UNREASONING GOES": The Comic Timing of Trembling', *Ill Seen Ill Said*, *Samuel Beckett Today*, vol. 11 (2001), pp. 373–81.
Samson, Andrea C., and James J. Gross, 'Humour as Emotion Regulation: The Differential Consequences of Negative Versus Positive Humour', *Cognition & Emotion*, vol. 26, no. 2 (2012), pp. 375–84.
Sanders, Barry, *Sudden Glory: Laughter as Subversive History* (Boston: Beacon Press, 1996).
Screech, Michael A., *Laughter at the Foot of the Cross* (Chicago: Chicago University Press, 2015).
Shakespeare, William, *The Norton Critical Edition*, ed. Stephen Greenblatt (London: Norton, 1997).
Small, Helen, 'The Bounded Life: Adorno, Dickens, and Metaphysics', *Victorian Literature and Culture*, vol. 32, no. 2 (2004), pp. 547–63.
Soble, Alan, 'Nothing Is Funy but Laughing Makes It So', *Philosophy Now*, no. 111 (December 2015/January 2016), pp. 8–10.
Speight, George, *The History of the English Puppet Theatre* (London: George G. Harrap, 1955).
Spencer, Herbert, 'The Physiology of Laughter', *Macmillan's Magazine*, no. 5 (March 1860), pp. 395–402.
Spencer, Lloyd, 'Introduction to Central Park', *New German Critique*, no. 34 (Winter 1985), pp. 28–31.
Stanhope, Phillip Dormer, *Letters Written by the Earl of Chesterfield to His Son* (New York: Derby and Jackson, 1897).
Stott, Andrew, *Comedy* (New York: Routledge, 2005).
Tambling, Jeremy, *Allegory and the Work of Melancholy: The Late Medieval and Shakespeare* (Amsterdam: Rodopi, 2004).
Tambling, Jeremy, *Hölderlin and the Poetry of Tragedy: Readings of Sophocles, Shakespeare, Nietzsche and Benjamin* (Eastbourne: Sussex University Press, 2014).
Tambling, Jeremy, *Literature and Psychoanalysis* (Manchester: Manchester University Press, 2012).
Terence, *The Comedies*, ed. and trans. Betty Radice (London: Penguin, 1976).
Thackeray, William Makepeace, *Vanity Fair*, ed. John Sutherland (Oxford: Oxford World's Classics, 1983).
Thomas, Jeannie B., *Featherless Chicken, Laughing Women and Serious Stories* (Virginia: University of Virginia Press, 1997).
Thompson, E. P., *The Making of the English Working Class* (Harmondsworth: Penguin, 1968).
Trahair, Lisa, *The Comedy of Philosophy: Sense and Nonsense in Early Cinematic Slapstick* (Albany: SUNY Press, 2007).
Vaillant, G. E., 'Adaptive Mental Mechanisms: Their Role in a Positive Psychology', *American Psychologist*, vol. 55 (2000), pp. 89–98.

Ver Eecke, Wilfreid, *Denial, Negation, and the Forces of the Negative* (Albany: SUNY Press, 2016).
Ver Eecke, Wilfreid, 'Hegel as Lacan's Source for Necessity in Psychoanalytic Theory', in *Interpreting Lacan*, ed. Joseph H. Smith and William Kerrigan (London: Yale, 1983), pp. 113–38.
Waller, John, 'Looking Back: Dancing Plagues and Mass Hysteria', *The Psychologist*, vol. 22, no. 7 (July 2009), pp. 644–7.
Weber, Samuel, *Benjamin's -Abilities* (Cambridge, MA: Harvard University Press, 2008).
Weber, Samuel, 'The Divaricator: Remarks on Freud's Witz', in *Glyph: Johns Hopkins Textual Studies 1* (Maryland: Johns Hopkins University Press, 1977), pp. 1–27.
Weber, Samuel, 'Laughter in the Meanwhile', *MLN*, vol. 102, no. 4, French issue (September 1987), pp. 691–706.
Weller, Shane, *Beckett, Literature and the Ethics of Alterity* (London: Palgrave Macmillan, 2006).
Žižek, Slavoj, *Event: Philosophy in Transit* (London: Penguin Books, 2014).
Žižek, Slavoj, *Less Than Nothing: Hegel and the Shadow of Dialectical Materialism* (London: Verso, 2012).
Zupančič, Alenka, *Ethics of the Real: Kant and Lacan* (London: Verso, 2011).
Zupančič, Alenka, *The Odd One In* (London: MIT Press, 2008).
Zupančič, Alenka, *The Shortest Shadow: Nietzsche's Philosophy of the Two* (Cambridge, MA: MIT Press, 2003).

Index